We Go High

We Go High

Nicole Ellis

Contents

*profiles detail trigger experiences.

Acknowledgments

I am eternally grateful for the many people who helped make this book possible. Thank you to all of the DK team including acquisitions editor Pete Jorgensen and my patient editor Elizabeth Cook. You are the best, even under immense pressure. I appreciate you. Jo Lightfoot for being my advocate and making this book a reality. My agents, Anthony Mattero and Traci Wilkes Smith—ya'll are truly the dream team. To my coach, counsel, confidant, and dear friend Jo-Ná Williams: thank you for being my north star and forcing me to always bet on myself. My father, Rodney Ellis, and my mother, Jacquelyn McLemore, thank you for being my biggest fans and the source of so many life lessons. My chosen family—The Calumet Country Club (you know who you are). To Karen McClain-Marvin, my trusted advisor, and mental health warrior. And my incredible team: Christine Ashley Forbes and Pauleanna Reid. Your talent is beyond measure. To the many family members, friends, and supporters that I didn't get to name, thank you for your love and support. I couldn't have done this without you.

Introduction

In 2010, I graduated college into a recession and moved in with my grandmother both out of necessity and a desire to do something I wouldn't dare say out loud at the time: go on a backpacking trip around the world by myself. With her support in the form of rent-free living and homecooked meals, I saved enough to pursue my life's dream at the time. During my 2-year solo journey through 25 countries, my greatest survival skill was to employ the lessons I'd learned at home as the daughter of stubborn Texans descended from a long line of stubborn, enslaved, afro-Texan women who spent most of their days picking cotton, and never got to experience the world beyond the box that slavery forced them into. The survival skills passed down through my own lineage and the lineages of women I had the pleasure of meeting around the world is the inspiration behind *We Go High*.

Some stories may be difficult for you to read, as they graphically detail racism, verbal and physical abuse, and potentially triggering experiences that are, unfortunately, relatable for many women—especially women of color, which is why I chose to include them.

My hope is that this book reminds you that you are not alone in the hills and valleys you come across in life. I hope that it gives you a few helpful tools and tactics for overcoming some of what you may face in your quest for respect, equality, visibility, and greatness. Every step forward will present new challenges that a woman of color somewhere else in the world is also dealing with. The pages that follow provide a catalogue of how a few women you may have heard of dealt with those challenges, and in many cases are still dealing with them. They are also a reminder that you can overcome these challenges, too.

Culture

Amanda Gorman

The rousing poet

Amanda Gorman made history on January 20th, 2021, when she became the youngest inaugural poet ever in the United States. At just 22, she joined the ranks of the linguistic greats, including Maya Angelo, Robert Frost, and Miller Williams.

On that historic day, she stood in front of the Capitol and the nation and spoke with an animated voice, filled with emotion. She described herself as a "skinny Black girl, descended from slaves and raised by a single mother," who can dream of being president one day, "only to find herself reciting for one." Her poem "The Hill We Climb," spoke deeply of loss and the fragile state of the nation. She also spoke of the possibility of a new day through unity, reconciliation, and bearing the weight of the full truth.

For Amanda, her truth can be found in her written words. She took to poetry at a young age as a result of a speech impediment. Rather than see it as an obstacle, Amanda took her difficulty with spoken word as an opportunity to strengthen her skills, mastering reading and writing at an early age. If she couldn't speak words to power, she would certainly write them.

Born and raised in Los Angeles, she quickly distinguished herself as a rising talent. In 2017, she became the first National Youth Poet Laureate in the United States, while also studying sociology at Harvard University.

Finding Inspiration

Two weeks before the inauguration, Amanda was struggling to string words together for her poem. Exhausted and overwhelmed she was concerned that she was not up to the monumental task. While it wasn't asked of her, it was the underlying assumption: this inauguration would need to bring together a divided nation, and her words were intended to be that bridge. Although she had written a few lines a day, the sentences weren't flowing, and her signature rhythm was missing. Then the Capitol Hill Riots happened. That night, she stayed up into the early hours of the morning, pouring all her unprocessed emotions into her journal. She described the apocalyptic scenes that had unfolded on that horrifying day.

On January 20th, 2021, her performance totally captivated the nation. It was an overcast day, with the sun occasionally peeking through the clouds. But what hung in the air was the tension building in the weeks prior to this day. Would there be a peaceful transition of power? No one would know until it was over. Following performances by Lady Gaga, Jennifer Lopez, and Garth Brooks, it was time for Amanda to share her words ...

Wearing a canary-yellow coat and a vibrant red headband, she stood and addressed a fractured country. With each verse and every stanza, she reminded every one of us that there was always light in the darkness; we just had to look for it.

"When day comes, we step out of the shade, aflame and unafraid.
The new dawn blooms as we free it.
For there is always light,
if only we're brave enough to see it.
If only we're brave enough to be it."

Prior to sharing the poem that would make her a household name, Amanda had been celebrated by notable women such as Hilary Clinton and Cynthia Erivo. Her career as a poet has in many ways been inspired by Malala Yousafazi, specifically by a speech given by Malala in 2013. At the age of 16 Amanda became a youth delegate for the United Nations. "It really opened my eyes to the possibilities of what I could accomplish," she said. Soon after, in 2014, she was named the inaugural Los Angeles Youth Poet Laureate. The following year, she published her first poetry collection, *The One for Whom Food Is Not Enough*.

Her future goals? Well back in 2017, long before she knew she would be performing at President Joe Biden's inauguration, she decided that she would run for office—the Oval Office. "This is a long, long, faraway goal, but in 2036 I am running for office to be president of the United States," she said matter-of-factly. "So you can put that in your iCloud calendar."

Kehlani

An artist in bloom

Turning 25 was more than a quarter-life milestone for Kehlani Ashley Parrish, it was a shock. "I always had a weird thing with being 25 or older," she says. "I'm now older than my father got to be." She was born in Oakland, California to a Spanish and Indigenous American mother and a Black American father. Much of her childhood was marked by trauma. She lost her father to substance abuse when she was a toddler. Soon after, her mother was incarcerated, and Kehlani bounced around foster care until her aunt dropped out of school to adopt her.

Among the turmoil, art became her saving grace. At 14, she enrolled at Oakland's School for the Arts. She had dreams of Julliard, but a knee injury in junior high forced her to switch from dance to music. One day, a classmate from the school's dance department suggested that she audition for a local cover band that was managed by his father D'wayne Wiggins, founding member of Tony! Toni! Toné! and brother to Raphael Saadiq. "I was hella scared," she admits. "It was the first time I really sang out. I sang to him and he was like, 'let's get it cracking.'"

She spent the next three years performing covers of classic soul records in the group alongside Wiggins' sons. Two years later, they auditioned for season six of *America's Got Talent*. The band placed fourth, however the excitement was short-lived. "There were a lot of contractual things that were going wrong and a lot of mistreatment from management.

The fact that we were 16—getting robbed and getting taken advantage of—was not OK," she said in an interview with *Complex*. "We had a meeting and [our managers] didn't expect me to come as correct as I did. I approached them with everything that was wrong on a list and said, 'This is not happening, this is not happening, and if this doesn't happen, I'm out of here.' They weren't willing to just be appropriate and professional." As a result, Kehlani decided to leave the band and pursue a career as a solo artist. She describes the next three years as a blur. "I went through a lot of growing up, being on the streets, being homeless, moving around, crib to crib, to crib. Just trying to graduate high school. Then Nick Cannon called me."

The Losses that Open Doors

He remembered her from her time on *America's Got Talent* and had an idea for a project in Los Angeles. "It ended up being this crazy rap group that I just wasn't down for," says Kehlani, who doesn't seem to realize how unusual it is to have such confidence in your own vision at such a young age. "That's for them, you wanna rap, go rap, feel me. I'm an R&B singer." Although the project didn't pan out, Kehlani had found a mentor in Nick.

She returned to Oakland solo and released "ANTISUMMERLUV" in the summer of 2013. Nick Cannon called again. "He called me and was like, 'Yo, I get your vision now! I get you, who you want to be as a solo artist. I respect it!'" She returned to LA under Nick's guidance. This time, he made sure she was taken care of.

"He's like, 'Yo, you can't be running around here trying to make music and you can't even think about music when you're worrying about what you're going to eat and where you're going to sleep,'" she says. "He comes at it from an uncle perspective. Just trying to make sure I'm alive and safe and healthy. So, he saved my life, and that's why I'm here today."

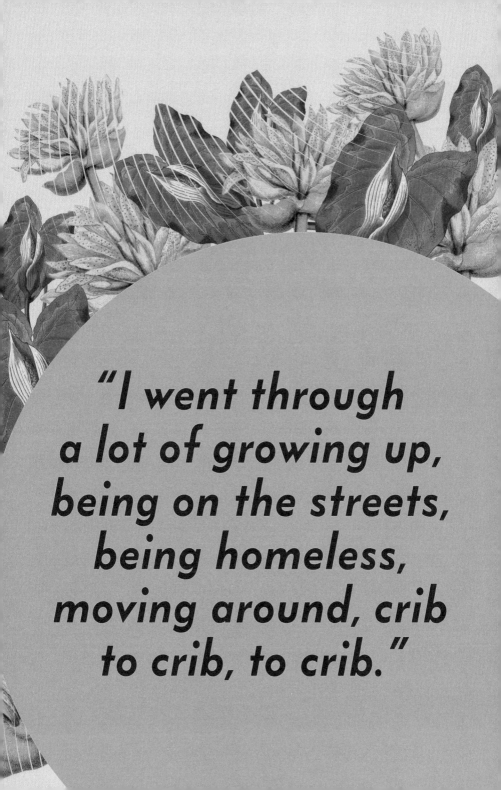

"I went through a lot of growing up, being on the streets, being homeless, moving around, crib to crib, to crib."

With Nick's support she was able to create *Cloud 19*, the 2014 album that would allow her to become a star on the rise. Her music was light, bubbly, and infectious. Shortly after, she was signed to Atlantic Records and released her second mixtape, *You Should Be Here*, which climbed to the top of Billboard's R&B charts and landed her a Grammy nomination. She was an artist in bloom.

Growing Pains

It felt overnight; blogs that had gushed over her sultry vocals were suddenly dissecting aspects of her personal life instead of focusing on the music she was sharing with the world.

In 2017, Kehlani pivoted to pop with the release of her debut album *SweetSexySavage*. While it received positive reviews on countless music blogs, the album lacked Kehlani's signatures and was completed during a personal mental-health crisis, that all but consumed.

"I started an album as one person and went through the most traumatic event in my life," she said. It wasn't an album she was prepared to release, but her label held fast to its deadline, leaving her to make an album when she could barely recognize herself. "I didn't connect with any of the music," she says. "I was embarrassed of everything."

"I started an album as one person and went through the most traumatic event in my life."

When it was time for her second album, she knew that she needed to create on her own terms and her own timeline. Then the pandemic happened, and her label balked at the idea of releasing an album when traditional means of marketing were impossible.

The planned videos were scrapped, and the album was put on hold. But Kehlani decided to give herself the green light and go ahead anyway. She released a lo-fi visual for "Toxic" on her MacBook and uploaded it. The label told her she was free to do what she wanted but she'd be on her own.

So she went to Best Buy, bought a camera, and taught herself Adobe Premiere Pro. Together with her photographer, she shot and released visuals for her third album. "People were more impressed with me shooting a video at my house than they were with me when I got a crazy-ass budget," she said.

The lesson for Kehlani was clear: when she acted in alignment with her authentic self, magic happened. Everything else was background noise.

Gabby Rivera

Telling your own stories

Gabby Rivera is a queer storyteller, self-proclaimed joy-advocate, and the first Latina to write for Marvel Comics. Her critically acclaimed debut novel *Juliet Takes a Breath* was listed by *Mic* as one of the 25 essential books to read for women's history month and called "f**king outstanding" by Roxane Gay. As an activist, Gabby's purpose is rooted in advancing the well-being of LGBTQ+ youth, particularly in minority communities—a purpose she's stayed committed to in all her written work. "When I'm here writing these stories and trying to figure out myself in my place and how I can interact and connect with my communities, I think of my grandmothers. I think of how they both believed in this country so much, and they both believed so deeply in the American dream," she said in an interview with *The Beacon*. "I don't care about white writer societies or mainstream or anything like that. We're going to be dikes, we're going to be queers, we're going to be in love, we're going to be happy, and we're going to live triumphantly to the end of our books and our movies, and that's *Juliet Takes a Breath*."

Joy as Action
Her career and love for literature began at the age of 17, where Gabby would often spend her evenings attending poetry slams at local cafes.

Eventually, she began performing on stage. Even in her earliest days as an artist, she drew her inspiration from stories written by Black, Brown, and queer artists, which allowed her to find belonging through the community.

> "You can't assume that everyone who's brown, beige, or likes rice and beans is Latinx, it's complicated."

Her literary novel, *Juliet Takes a Breath*, is a semiautobiographical coming-of-age novel about a gay Latinx woman learning to fall in love with her identity. The book addresses important issues of representation and intergenerational cultural differences by exploring the relationship between the main character, Juliet Milagros Palante, and her white feminist boss, Harlow Brisbane. Ultimately, the story is set to remind young readers to trust in their own power and create space for themselves in both Latinx and feminist communities.

Gabby continued to teach through her writing at Marvel Comics. Between 2017-2018 she penned the solo-series *America*, a comic about America Chavez, a 19-year-old Latinx girl who has the ability to travel through different portals and dimensions. "I wanted America Chavez to be like a safe and gentle place where people, especially young people of color, could pick up the comic, and be like, 'Oh I feel loved, I feel cared for, I don't feel stressed.' I don't want to create art that harms my people and my communities," said Gabby.

Healing Through Stories

In true Gabby fashion, she created a series that not only acted as a safe space for marginalized youth but also expanded what was possible.

"You can't assume that everyone who's brown, beige, or likes rice and beans is Latinx, it's complicated," she said. But she also wanted her writing to heal those that have suffered and hold those that caused harm in the real world accountable through fiction.

The villains in her comics were modeled after the white supremacists in Charlottesville. "I didn't have to make this up, it was just me trying to grapple with what I see all around me, and the ways that they [white men] present themselves as aggressive and violent toward us," she said. "To everybody who in any way can connect with America Chavez, I offer peace and the right to sit in the sun. You do not have to keep up with capitalism, you do not have to keep up with a routine that doesn't serve you, or doesn't serve your joy. And when everything is painful, you still have the right to sit in the sun and heal."

"Your work is to heal, to love yourself,
to find all the things that you need
to say and say to them when it feels right."

Her focus is on healing herself and those who recognize themselves in her work. She hopes to remind the LGBTQ+ community, especially those who identify as Latinx, that their journey is theirs alone. "Your family [and] your relatives have to go on their own journey and that is not your work as much as you probably feel like it is. Your work is to heal, to love yourself, to find all the things that you need to say and say to them when it feels right, but your job is not to meet anybody's hand through your queerness."

Politics

Stacey Abrams

Creating strategy out of setbacks

On a breezy November night in Georgia, Stacey Abrams made her way across the stage in a purple blazer to a podium carrying a matching purple campaign poster with her name on it. The sign said: STACEY ABRAMS GOVERNOR.

Abrams' 2018 run for Governor of Georgia made her the first Black American woman to become a major-party gubernatorial nominee in the United States. Her loss was one of the most widely reported instances of voter suppression in American history. For others, this might have been the end of a career in politics. For Abrams, it marked the beginning of an even bigger mission to make sure every eligible adult in America is able to exercise their right to vote. Within two years she created the most influential initiative to fight voter suppression in the country and founded a coalition of nonprofits to register over a million Georgians to vote in elections for years to come.

Barriers & Bias

Like most women of color, Abrams is familiar with barriers to access. This was not even the first time Abrams had been held back when trying to reach the Governor's Mansion. When she was made the first Black valedictorian of her high school, Abrams and her family were invited to a dinner for the state's top students at the Governor's Mansion. The family traveled by bus, as they could not afford a car. Seeing this, a guard insisted they didn't belong at this private party. Her parents pushed back and the family were admitted. Abrams doesn't remember the party, meeting her fellow valedictorians, the governor, or anything else from that day except being turned away at the door.

> *"I want to be the person who says those gates are open for everyone because no one should be denied access because of their circumstances."*

From Struggle to Strategy

Abrams' recollection and response to being singled out in high school is one of many examples of how she processes adversity. She has felt the pain and trauma of being undervalued, overlooked, and excluded based on skin color, gender, and income. Once that initial sting subsides, she pivots to analyzing the problem, the contributing factors, and above all, herself to decide how to change it. In this case, it was to one day show the state, and the country, that she deserved to be at the Governor's Mansion by running for governor.

This hallmark trait of leveraging setbacks is laid bare in every aspect of her life, including money. One of six children growing up in a low-income household, Abrams frequently bore the responsibility of financially supporting her family. With little access to financial literacy or capital, Abrams still had $200,000 in debt during her gubernatorial run in 2018—$50,000 in deferred taxes and $170,000 in credit card and student loan debt.

Abrams recognized she was not alone in this struggle, noting in an article for *Fortune*: "Debt is a millstone that weighs down more than three quarters of Americans … It should not—and cannot—be a disqualification for ambition." Abrams first began taking on considerable debt to go to college and graduate school. The risk seemingly paid off when she landed her first job after graduating from Yale Law School. Her salary was $95,000, three times her parents' income combined. However, as Abrams began to pay off those debts, even bigger financial obligations emerged. Hurricane Katrina battered her parents' community, leaving Abrams to be the breadwinner and provider for her family again. Abrams' financial strain was exacerbated further when her parents became responsible for her brother's newborn daughter.

> *"Every time I wanted to make a leap deciding to run for office, I had to think about what that would mean for all of the people who rely on me."*

Rather than cast light away from her financial challenges, Abrams put them front and center in her campaign for governor, pointing out that race and gender play a major role in determining just how big of a financial disadvantage we're likely to face. Understanding the systemic nuances of how and why she found herself thousands of dollars in debt, Abrams used her platform to encourage financial literacy and advise others about what they can learn from her experiences.

Abrams' unrelenting dedication to deconstructing the barriers she experienced growing up led her to pursue a career in politics in 2006 as the State Representative for Georgia's 89th district. Growing up with Methodist pastors as parents, Abrams knew how to connect with congregations of all sorts, including policy makers and voters. She brought everything learned in church to the halls of the Georgia State Capitol—whittling big ideas and political jargon down to the basics of how policies effect the everyday lives of the people she represented. She was so skilled, her fellow representatives on both sides of the aisle would ask her to review their bills before presenting them.

In 2014, Abrams created the New Georgia Project, a voter registration program to make voting more accessible to people of color ahead of the senate election that same year. Abrams led the organization part-time while still holding office. The small but ambitious organization registered roughly 69,000 new voters in its first year.

In 2017, Abrams stepped down as minority leader to run for Governor. Her opponent, then Secretary of State Brian Kemp was in charge of voter registration. In July 2017, Kemp purged more than 500,000 voter registrations, the largest mass disenfranchisement in US history. Between 2012 and 2018, Kemp canceled 1.4 million voter registrations, using tactics that date back to American Jim Crow laws. In most elections, a winner is decided within 24 hours of election day. For Abrams, this process took ten days. She describes the days between the election and formally stepping out of the race as compounding stages of grief hitting her all at once. Voter suppression hotlines managed by her campaign and nonprofits banked over 80,000 calls from Georgians whose ballots were not counted, or whose names were purged from the voting roles. "Until this election, I had never considered myself an angry person," Abrams would later write.

Propelling Pain
By the sixth day, still in the heat of a legal battle, Abrams again pivoted to analyze the root of the problem to decide what to do next. Still grieving, she decided to add another stage to the mourning process.

It's called plotting. Some of us heal through a drawn-out grieving process that ends in acceptance. In Abrams' case, accepting defeat also meant accepting inequality. Plotting offered a new path where healing and making the difference you want to see in the world can make perceived failures integral to future successes. She grabbed the nearest legal pad and began to write out what would later become a coalition of organizations dedicated to ending voter suppression, disenfranchisement, and inequality. Abrams' newly reclaimed purpose made her path forward clearer than ever despite being in the midst of an unbearable loss.

On November 16, 2018, Abrams ascended the stage one last time as America's first female Black American gubernatorial candidate not to concede, but to announce the beginning of a mission to uphold a right her enslaved ancestors died fighting for: the right to vote.

Despite narrowly losing to Governor Kemp, Abrams received more votes than any Democrat in Georgia election history, including President Barack Obama and Hillary Clinton during their presidential campaigns. Abrams' run became an inflection point for voter turnout among Latinx, Asian, and Black American voters.

"Winning doesn't always mean you get the prize. Sometimes you get progress."

That progress would serve a multitude of purposes through the creation of Fair Fight Action and Fair Fight PAC to tackle voter suppression, Fair Count to address the census and beyond, and the Southern Economic Advancement Project, and bolstering New Georgia Project's voter registration drives. For Abrams, winning a single election is not a victory; ensuring that every election is a true reflection of the will of the people is.

Kamala Harris

The first but not the last

Vice President Kamala Devi Harris knew she was going to be a part of something bigger than herself when she accepted the inauguration oath. She was standing on the shoulders of giants, and she had every intention of taking them with her as she took that oath. "I will be thinking about my mother, who is looking down from heaven," Kamala said in an interview. "I will be thinking about all of the people who are counting on us to lead and are counting on us to see them and to address their needs and the things that keep them up at night. And I'll be thinking about the fact that we have to hit the ground running immediately to support the people of our country, to support the children of our country, and to help get us out of the crises that we're facing."

On January 20th, 2021, Kamala became America's first female, Black, and Indian American vice president. Growing up, her mother would often tell her, "Kamala, you may be the first to do many things, but make sure you are not the last." Her mother was right. "I hope that by being a 'first,' I inspire young people to pursue their dreams," she said.

"The number of times that I've heard the word 'no'—or that something can't be done—in my lifetime is too many to count."

A Vice President for the People

She was born in Oakland, California, to immigrant parents. Her mother, Shyamala Gopalan, was a breast cancer scientist and a pioneer in her own right. Her father, Donald J. Harris, was an economics professor at Stanford University. The couple met through the civil rights movement, and raised their children with a tenacity for justice.

"I'm honored to be considered a 'first,' but I always think about the people who came before and paved the way for me to get where I am today."

"My parents would bring me to protests strapped tightly in my stroller, and my mother, Shyamala, raised my sister, Maya, and me to believe that it was up to us and every generation of Americans to keep on marching," Harris said during her first campaign appearance as the Democratic nominee for vice president. "She'd tell us 'Don't sit around and complain about things; do something.' So I did something. I devoted my life to making real the words carved in the United States Supreme Court: Equal justice under law."

Through every step of her career, Kamala has fought for the people. In 1990, she began her legal career at the Alameda County District Attorney's Office where she specialized in prosecuting child sexual assault cases. She then served as a managing attorney in the San Francisco District Attorney's Office, and later was chief of

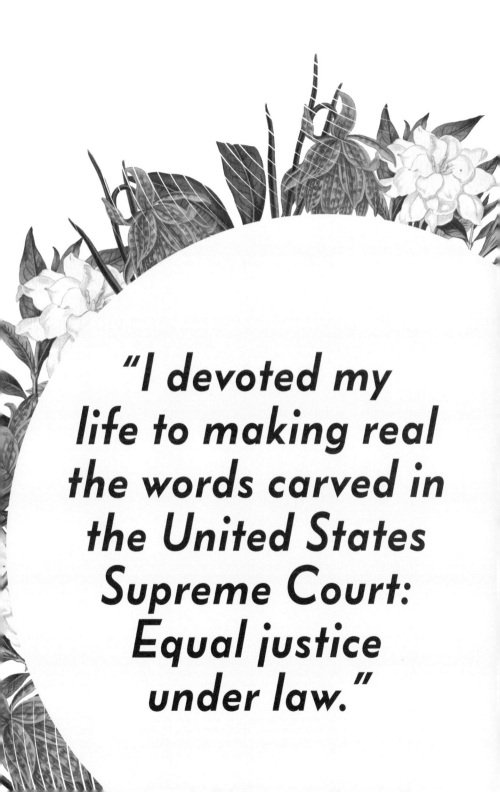

"I devoted my life to making real the words carved in the United States Supreme Court: Equal justice under law."

the Division on Children and Families for the San Francisco City Attorney's Office. In 2003, she was elected District Attorney of San Francisco.

In her time as the DA, she created a groundbreaking program that provided first-time drug offenders with the opportunity to earn a high school degree and find employment. The program was designated as a national model of innovation for law enforcement by the United States Department of Justice. Then, in 2010, Kamala was elected California's Attorney General and oversaw the largest state justice department in the United States. She established the state's first Bureau of Children's Justice and instituted several first-of-their-kind reforms that ensured greater transparency and accountability in the criminal justice system.

As Attorney General Vice President Harris won a $20 billion settlement for Californians whose homes had been foreclosed on, as well as a $1.1 billion settlement for students and veterans who were taken advantage of by a for-profit education company. She defended the Affordable Care Act in court, enforced environmental law, and was a national leader in the movement for marriage equality. In 2016 Kamala Harris was elected to the US Senate.

Being in Your Power

Although Kamala has the accolades, the experience, and the repertoire, there was pushback when she announced her candidacy for presidency in 2018. For the soon-to-be vice president, it was nothing new. "I have in my career been told many times, 'It's not your time,' 'It's not your turn.' Let me just tell you, I eat 'no' for breakfast. So, I would recommend the same," Kamala declared.

During the first Democratic presidential debate in June 2019, Kamala criticized former vice president Joe Biden for hurtful remarks he made, speaking fondly of senators who opposed integration efforts in the 1970s and working with them to oppose mandatory school bussing (the practice of transporting students to schools in different neighborhoods in an effort to address racial segregation). Her support rose between 6-9 points after that debate. It was clear early on that she was comfortable asking the tough questions; it's always been a part of her brand. "Anyone who claims to be a leader must speak like a leader. That means speaking with integrity and truth," Kamala said. Although she eventually withdrew her candidacy for presidency, she had left an impression. It was clear that Kamala Harris was the leader America needed.

On August 11th, 2020, Joe Biden announced that his running mate would be Kamala Harris. Five months later, they would come together to lead a fractured nation.

Vice President Kamala Harris was sworn-in by Associate Supreme Court Justice Sonia Sotomayor, her left hand resting on two Bibles held by her husband, Doug Emhoff. The one on top was a Bible used by the late Supreme Court Justice Thurgood Marshall. The second Bible belonged to the late Regina Shelton, a woman Harris considered a "second mother" who babysat her and her sister Maya whenever their mother worked late in the lab at U.C. Berkeley.

To the young people watching her at home, Kamala had a clear message:

"Dream with ambition, lead with conviction, and see yourself in a way that others might not see you, simply because they've never seen it before."

Michelle Obama

When they go low, we go high

When Michelle LaVaughn Robinson arrived at the doors of Princeton University, she immediately felt marked by otherness, and the weight of her identity. "If in high school I'd felt as if I were representing my neighborhood, now at Princeton I was representing my race. Anytime I found my voice in class or nailed an exam, I quietly hoped it helped make a larger point," she wrote in her autobiography, *Becoming*.

Her experiences told her that she belonged, but the world outside of her wasn't so sure. In high school, she had graduated in the top ten percent of her class, with an impressive list of extracurriculars. But when she told her high school guidance counsellor, she was considering Princeton for college, she was met with skepticism.

"It's possible, in fact, that during our short meeting the college counselor said things to me that might have been positive and helpful, but I recall none of it," she wrote. "Because rightly or wrongly, I got stuck on one single sentence the woman uttered. 'I'm not sure,' she said, giving me a perfunctory, patronizing smile, 'that you're Princeton material.'"

Despite the fact that she had skipped the second grade and been admitted into a school for gifted children. Or the fact that she had come from a family that prioritized education, and that her older brother was already studying at Princeton. The rhetoric was relentless: she did not belong in prestigious academic institutions. Or so they tried to tell her.

She disregarded her college counsellor, blocking the memory from her mind and applied anyway. Seven months later, she received her acceptance letter.

"I never did stop in on the college counselor to tell her she'd been wrong—that I was Princeton material after all. It would have done nothing for either of us."

When They Go Low, We Go High

The doubt that consumed her during her first few months at Princeton dissipated altogether by her sophomore year. That's when the reality of the Ivy League began sinking in: overwhelmingly white, and male. She was unimpressed.

"I'm expecting brilliance. Genius," Michelle told *CBS This Morning* cohost Gayle King. "And then what I discover is, wow, there's a lot of arbitrariness to this stuff, you know? There's a debate about affirmative action when it comes to race. What I point out is that when I got to Princeton, I realized there's ... all kinds of affirmative action that goes on. There are kids who get in because they're athletes. There are kids who get in because there's a legacy. It's just that race stands out. ... But it was important for me to see that." From an early age, the future First Lady had consistently shown an ability to block out dissenting voices and follow her inner compass.

It was that tenacity that earned her a seat at Harvard Law School and a job offer at one of the world's most prestigious law firms—Sidley Austin. It was there, as a second-year associate that she met the man who would become her husband and the 44th president of the United States of America.

"There's a debate about affirmative action when it comes to race."

Owning Her Mark: Becoming the First Lady

In the eight years that Michelle Obama spent in the White House, she left behind an unprecedented legacy and reshaped how many understood the influence of the First Lady. Although she gracefully took to the role and made it her own, when Barack first shared the idea of running for president, she was understandably reluctant. The couple had two small children, and political life was rarely, if ever, family friendly. Slowly she transitioned from hesitant spouse to a fierce defender of her husband's policies and a political force in her own right.

From the earliest moments of her public life, she made it clear she had no interest in fitting into molds others had created for her. When asked on the campaign trail what kind of First Lady she would be, her most common response was "I won't know until I get there."

Following the historical 2008 win, Michelle began to bloom in her role. Still somewhat reluctant, and somewhat unsure, she made clear that she was not just another First Lady. Her first major project was planting a new garden on the South Lawn of the White House in 2009. This would serve as the starting point of her Let's Move! initiative the following year, where she took on childhood obesity and lack of access to healthy food. This project was a complement to one of the Obama administration's biggest domestic projects—health care reform.

In 2009, Michelle became one of the few First Ladies able to get legislation passed. She called the Healthy, Hunger-Free Kids Act a cornerstone of her work during the first year of the Let's Move! initiative. The act served to update school meal nutritional standards, offer healthier meal options for students, and increase the number of students who had access to school lunch at little or no cost. Ultimately, it was her authenticity and outreach to the private sector around nutritional labels and food that had the greatest impact.

Of course, there were critics from both ends of the political spectrum. Some believed she worked too closely with big corporations. Others argued that she was encouraging government overreach onto their children's plates.

But long before she was the First Lady, she was a mother who cared about her kids' health. Just like when she was a student at Princeton, she remained focused on her vision and her purpose, and blocked out those who could not see the future she envisioned.

This wasn't about politics; it was about the well-being of children and the future of the nation. So, she dug deep and went high, using social media to post workout videos and inspire young people at home to take ownership of their health—and it worked.

Lifting As You Climb

Toward the end of her husband's presidency, she began to speak more candidly about the challenges of being the country's first Black American First Lady. "I was also the focus of another set of questions and speculations, conversation sometimes rooted in the fears and misperceptions of others. Was I too loud or too angry or too emasculating?" she told the graduating class at historically Black Tuskegee University.

She's also talked about how it felt to be mocked on the cover of *The New Yorker*. "It was a cartoon drawing of me with a huge Afro and a machine gun," Michelle said. "Now, it was satire, but if I'm really being honest, it knocked me back a bit." This type of bullying was not new to her. It was the same tactics she endured in high school, at Princeton, and even at Harvard. But in true First Lady fashion, when they went low, she still went high.

"You reach back, and you give other folks the same chances that helped you succeed."

Rather than shrink at the words of bullies, she used each and every opportunity to inspire young Black women around the world by teaching so many of us how to handle those who are uncomfortable with a woman in power.

"When you've worked hard, and done well, and walked through that doorway of opportunity, you do not slam it shut behind you," she wrote.

STEM and Business

Arundhati Bhattacharya

An inspiring businesswoman

When Arundhati Bhattacharya was a little girl, she watched her neighbor die. The community she lived in did not have adequate medical care, which meant people would regularly fall ill. After the untimely death, Arundhati remembers her mother spending night after night studying homeopathic medicine so that the next time a neighbor fell ill, she would be able to help.

Her mother refused to sit by and let another loved one pass because of a lack of knowledge or service. "She even ran a clinic until three months before her death. I learned from her that when faced with a situation, act! There is no point in sitting back," she recalled. This is a lesson that Arundhati attributes to having shaped her life and career trajectory.

She's often celebrated for single-handedly saving the State Bank of India from the brink of collapse. At a time when bankers and financial institutions invited skepticism and mistrust, she inspired confidence. Initially, she joined the State Bank of India as a probationary officer. She was 22.

Throughout her 36-year career with the bank, she's worked in foreign exchange, treasury, retail operations, human resources, and investment banking. Additionally, she's also served at the bank's New York office. During her time at the bank, she introduced a two year sabbatical leave policy for the bank's female employees to use for maternity leave or elder care. Under her leadership, female employees were also offered free vaccinations against cervical cancer.

> "When faced with a situation, act!
> There is no point in sitting back."

In 2016, *Forbes* magazine ranked her as one of the 25 Most Powerful Women in the World. She has also been recognized as one of the top 100 Global Thinkers by *Foreign Policy Magazine* and is number 26 on *Fortune's* World 50 Greatest Leaders list.

Arundhati began her career as one of the few Indian women in her field, but that didn't stop her from becoming the first woman to lead a Fortune 500 company in India.

How She Did It

Born into a Bengali family in Kolkata, India, Arundhati spent her childhood watching her parents work tirelessly to make ends meet and give back to their community. She attributes much of her success and work ethic to her upbringing, citing both her mother and a close aunt as role models. She attended St. Xavier's School, Bokaro, and studied English literature at Kolkata's Lady Brabourne College and Jadavpur University. Upon graduation, her career accelerated because she needed it to. Her father retired unexpectedly. Aware of her family's financial hardships, young Arundhati decided that she needed to become financially independent, to alleviate her family's financial strain. "My father retired from the Steel Authority of India without a pension, so I wanted to be self-reliant quickly," she said. Running on determination and necessity, Arundhati worked hard and in 1977 joined the State Bank of India - beginning the career that would make her a household name. Quickly climbing the ranks, she surpassed expectations and shattered glass ceilings.

Set Up to Fail

Many tried to stop her; she was often left out of meetings, ignored, and denied opportunities readily available to her male counterparts. Instead of staying silent and accepting what was happening, she spoke out and fiercely advocated for herself and other women in the workplace. She recalls one incident in particular, where she was appointed chief general manager for a new project. From the beginning, she knew that she was being set up to fail. "Nobody thought I could pull off the project, but it turned out to be a rewarding one and brought me great learning and satisfaction. There are always ways to turn setbacks around," she said. "My mentor advised me not to give up before I had exhausted all possibilities. Giving up is easier, one shouldn't take the easy option out."

In 2020, Arundhati left the world of banking for a new role as the CEO of Salesforce India. In 18-months, she transformed the work environment. Now, it's recognized as one of India's best companies to work for.

"Giving up is easier; one shouldn't take the easy option out."

Whether it's in banking, IT or advocating for women's rights, what makes Arundhati such an inspiring force is her ability to constantly go beyond the limits others place on her. It's what's made her truly unstoppable.

Dr. Kizzmekia Corbett

Viral immunologist

M any of us awaited the end of 2020 with bated breath. News headlines were flooded with talks of a possible vaccine, signaling a potential end to a pandemic that had already stolen too much from us. Yet for many there was hesitance. Was the vaccine safe?

During a Q&A with the National Urban Justice League, Dr. Anthony Fauci, the nation's top infectious disease expert was asked about the input of Black American scientists in the vaccine development process.

There was no hesitation in his response.

"The very vaccine that's one of the two that has absolutely exquisite levels—94 to 95% efficacy against clinical disease and almost 100% efficacy against serious disease that are shown to be clearly safe—that vaccine was actually developed in my institute's vaccine research center by a team of scientists led by Dr. Barney Graham and his close colleague, Dr. Kizzmekia Corbett, or Kizzy Corbett," Dr. Fauci told the forum. "Kizzy is an African American scientist who is right at the forefront of the development of the vaccine."

Not Another Hidden Figure

Kizzmekia "Kizzy" Shanta Corbett is an American viral immunologist, the Shutzer Assistant Professor at the Harvard Radcliffe Institute and Assistant Professor of Immunology and Infectious Diseases at Harvard T.H. Chan School of Public Health. Prior to joining the faculty at Harvard, she spent six years at the Vaccine Research Center and the National Institute of Allergy and Infectious Diseases, National Institutes of Health in Bethesda, Maryland. She earned her PhD in microbiology and immunology from the University of North Carolina at Chapel Hill. Prior to the pandemic, Kizzy's research focused on developing vaccines for other coronaviruses, in partnership with Moderna.

Soon that research became even more vital. Just a few weeks after it originated in China, the novel coronavirus was ravaging through communities all around the world, shutting down national economies and sending city after city into frightful lockdowns. On March 25th, 2020, the President declared a national emergency and news channels followed with grim predictions from leading experts, warning of a virus unlike anything known in modern history. The public was told to brace itself for up to two years of lockdowns. What they did not know was that in a lab deep inside the National Institutes of Health, a group of scientists were already working on a vaccine. Dr. Kizzy was one of the lead immunologists. By the time the United States issued a state of

"Kizzy is an African American scientist who is right at the forefront of the development of the vaccine."

Dr. Fauci

emergency, she had already begun designing animal tests of the vaccine and coordinating means of measuring its effectiveness in humans.

At just 33 years old, the remarkable scientist was well known within her field for her extraordinary combination of drive, dedication, and optimism. When it came to predicting the first public immunization, she had her eyes on April 2021. Instead, the rollout began four months earlier. When a New York City intensive-care nurse received the first shot, a beaming Fauci praised the then-unknown scientist as someone who would go down in history as a key player in developing the science that could end the pandemic.

For Dr. Kizzy, watching the first dose of the Moderna vaccine being administered was indescribable. It was more than a career milestone; she was saving lives.

Paying It Forward: Building with Community

In 25 years at Oak Lane Elementary School, teacher Myrtis Bradsher had never seen a child like Kizzy Corbett. She was always put together, with her hair adorned with ribbons that matched her outfits. But that wasn't what drew the fourth-grade teacher to Kizzy. "She had so much knowledge," the teacher recalled. "She knew something about everything." Always quick to finish her own work, Kizzy would often rush to help other fourth-graders with their schoolwork. Even at a young age, she found joy in helping others learn.

Myrtis was one of the few Black teachers at the elementary school and she pushed to give young Kizzy the advantages she knew she deserved. At a parent-teacher conference, she told Kizzy's parents just that. "Look," she recalled saying to Kizzy's mother, Rhonda Brooks, "she's so far above other children. We need to send her to a class for exceptional students. I need you to say we have your permission." That decision ultimately put Kizzy on the path that led her to the National Institutes of Health and the development of the Moderna vaccine.

"I didn't know Kizzy had gone that far until recently," said Myrtis, now 72 and retired. "I figured she would, but I thought I probably would never hear about it." Kizzy's brilliance has always been undeniable. It's also a testament to the fact that it takes a village. In the words of Toni Morisson, "When you get these jobs that you have been so brilliantly trained for, just remember that your real job is that if you are free, you need to free somebody else. If you have some power, then your job is to empower somebody else. This is not just a grab-bag candy game."

The pandemic gave her an opportunity to do exactly that.

"Vaccines have the potential to be the equalizer of health disparities, especially around infectious diseases."

Taking the Lead

Covid-19 magnified the impact of racial and wealth disparity in America. Across the nation, Black and Brown communities were disproportionately affected by coronavirus, according to the US Centers for Disease Control and Prevention (CDC). Getting the vaccine into communities of color was crucial, and to Dr. Kizzy, it was also deeply personal.

In a survey conducted in 2020 by the CDC, 46% of Black adults said they probably would not get vaccinated against the coronavirus SARS-CoV-2, compared with 30% of white respondents. Those who were hesitant cited concerns relating to side effects, and the speed at which the vaccines were developed. This discrepancy can likely be explained by historical and ongoing medical racism, such as the infamous syphilis studies in Tuskegee, Alabama—in which doctors withheld treatment from hundreds of Black men from the 1930s to the 1970s.

Seeing these numbers, Dr. Kizzy decided there was more work to be done. "Vaccines have the potential to be the equalizer of health disparities, especially around infectious diseases," said Dr. Kizzy. "I could never sleep at night if I developed anything—if any product of my science came out—and it did not equally benefit the people that look like me. Period."

She began to speak at churches, community centers, and all over social media, answering questions and easing concerns. The message was clear— a person who looks like you has been developing this vaccine for several years. "For a long time, we left the general public on the outside of vaccine development, until it was time to give them their shot. And that's just unacceptable," said Dr. Kizzy.

"If I never talked to anybody in the community, if I never cared whether vaccines got into anyone's arms, I could still be a very notable scientist. But that doesn't sit well with me."

Mae Jemison

The sky isn't the limit

Mae Jemison was 16 years old when she was admitted to Stanford University. It was 1973 and she was one of just a handful of Black students enrolled in the school's engineering program. "Some professors would just pretend I wasn't there," she said, in an interview with *The New York Times*. "I would ask a question and a professor would act as if it was just so dumb, the dumbest question he had ever heard. Then, when a white guy would ask the same question, the professor would say, 'That's a very astute observation.'" The criticism was constant, and the praise was few and far in between. "As a medical student, sometimes I needed to hear the criticism in order to become a good doctor. Also, as an engineer, and as an astronaut. But many times, what's lacking is the praise," she said. The negative remarks that often followed Mae from classroom to classroom weren't based on her performance or her abilities; they were based on race.

"Race is always an issue in the United States," she commented. "You always run into people who aren't comfortable with you. But we all—the way people look, whether or not they're heavyset, for example, influences us. Anyone who says he isn't influenced by race is lying." Rather than shy away and make herself small, she learned how to filter the comments that would help her grow, and leave the rest.

Following a Dream

Mae Jemison is possibly one of the most impressive people you will ever encounter. She is the first Black American woman to be admitted into NASA's astronaut training program. She holds a bachelor's degree in chemical engineering and African studies from Stanford University, and a medical degree from Cornell University. She is an author, Peace Corp volunteer, teacher, actress, accomplished dancer, and the founder of two technology companies.

The youngest of three children, Mae was born in Decatur, Alabama, but moved to Chicago, Illinois, at the age of three. "As a little girl ... I always assumed I would go into space," she said in an interview with *New Scientist*. "Let me make sure that's clear: I just always assumed, despite the fact that the US hadn't sent any women up there, or people of color, that I was going to go." She would also one day become the first real astronaut to appear in an episode of *Star Trek*.

"In kindergarten my teacher asked me—actually asked the whole class—now what do you want to be when you grow up? And I said, 'I want to be a scientist,'" recounted May. "And she looked at me and she said, 'Don't you mean a nurse?' Now clearly, there is no issue with being a nurse. But the issue back then was, that's the only thing she could see a little girl growing up to do, that had something to do with sciences." Mae remembers putting her hands on her hips, and firmly telling her teacher no, she didn't mean nurse—she meant scientist.

"In kindergarten my teacher asked me—actually asked the whole class—now what do you want to be when you grow up? And I said, 'I want to be a scientist.'"

Curiosity That Made History

Mae was excited about the world around her. Everything from fishing or hunting with her father, to playing in the sun with her siblings would fill her with a sense of purpose and wonder. It's this sense of adventure and endless possibility that drew her to science. After graduating from Stanford University, she chose to attend medical school, satiating her constant desire to learn and understand the human condition. While studying at Cornell Medical school, she worked in Kenya, Cuba, and at a Cambodian refugee camp in Thailand. Shortly after graduating, she was a Peace Corp medical officer for Sierra Leone and Liberia, where she also taught and conducted medical research.

She returned to the United States in 1985 and chose to follow in the footsteps of Sally Ride, who in 1983, became the first American woman in space. That year, over 2,000 people applied to NASA's astronaut training program. Only 15 people were accepted, and Mae became the first Black American woman ever to be admitted into the program.

On September 12, 1992, Mae Jemison became the first Black woman to travel into space. She served as a mission specialist aboard space shuttle *Endeavour*.

Mae Jemison has repeatedly made history by following her curiosity and allowing herself to follow her heart. Throughout her life, she has faced challenges and setbacks that attempted to rob her of her passion. Every time she was faced with an overwhelming obstacle, she chose not to fold. Her accolades are a testament to what happens when you choose to keep moving forward in the face of adversity.

On September 12, 1992, Mae Jemison became the first Black woman to travel into space.

Angelica Ross

The algorithm of authenticity

Angelica always knew she was different; she just didn't have the words for it. At 17, she left her hometown of Racine, Wisconsin, to begin a new life in Rochester, New York. In between waiting tables at chain restaurants, she found herself doing drag at local clubs. It was there that she met Miss Armani. "As we were changing in the dressing room, I noticed that she had real breasts," she said. "Until that very moment, I had no idea I could actually change my body to match how I felt on the inside. It was a revelation, but not necessarily one I was ready to have."

Rather than accept herself, Angelica enlisted in the Navy. She hoped it would turn her straight, or at the very least toughen her up. It was 1999 —the era of Don't Ask, Don't Tell, an act that prohibited any gay men, bisexuals, or lesbians from disclosing their sexual orientation or speaking about any same-sex relationships, while serving in the United States armed forces. Despite her bleached blonde hair and red toenails, she was accepted after basic training and stationed in Japan. The rumors about her started shortly after. One night, Angelica was invited to a party in the barracks. When she arrived, she distinctly remembers hearing the door lock behind her as she entered. She looked around and saw about 15 Navy men and women staring back at her.

"Are you really gay?"

"We don't care, we just want to know."

Afraid and alone, she kept denying her sexuality. Then one of the guys grabbed her by the shirt and said, "Admit you're gay or I'm going to punch you in the face right now!" So, she did. But the violence was just beginning. He grabbed her and flipped her upside down and hung her out of the third story window. As the blood began pooling at the tips of her flailing arms and the top of her head, she thought she was going to die. When he finally pulled her back inside, she sprinted to the door and didn't look back. The next day, she was called to the captain's office and told it was time for her to leave. "I'd been warned by my so-called friend not to tell him what had really happened, so instead, I signed a document saying that I'm 'an admitted homosexual' and was discharged—not as honorable or dishonorable, but as 'uncharacterized'—leaving me without benefits or access to the GI bill," she recalled.

"Discrimination is a part of any trans person's life."

Choosing to Live Out Loud

After leaving the Navy, Angelica decided it was time to live her truth. she didn't have any money, an education, or support, but what she did have was clarity. For the first time in her life, she knew who she was. Even if the world wasn't ready for her yet, she could no longer afford the alternative. She changed her name to Angelica; got a Whitney Houston–style weave; and, whenever her budget allowed it, she bought black-market hormones from her friends. "Discrimination is a part of any trans person's life," she said. "Ninety percent of us report workplace harassment or mistreatment and nearly half of us have been fired from, or passed over for, jobs because of our gender identity, according to a recent study. Trans people of color, in particular, are up to four times more likely to be unemployed than the general population." Angelica was fired from nearly every job she'd ever had. "Later, I worked as a waitress, but after I objected to the harassment I was getting in the kitchen and to being called by my male birth name, I got fired from that job, too," she recalled.

> *"I believe that other people can have a PhD level in understanding themselves."*

The Power of Alignment

Something happened when Angelica decided to be her authentic self. Every single time a door closed, five more opened for her. After losing yet another job, she moved to Florida. A friend had promised her a job at an adult website in exchange for cash for hormones and implants. But she quickly realized this was not the work she was wanted to do and decided to redesign the entire website herself, learning code and graphic design along the way. She was Angelica Ross, and she had something powerful to offer the world, with or without a degree.

"I tell folks: 'Even though I don't have a degree, I have a PhD in Ms. Ross.' And I believe that other people can have a PhD level in understanding themselves," she said. "You don't have to think, 'I don't have a bachelor's degree, I don't have this certification' or whatnot, you can curate your own learning that is specific to who you are, to what your passions are, to whatever transitional phase you are in life."

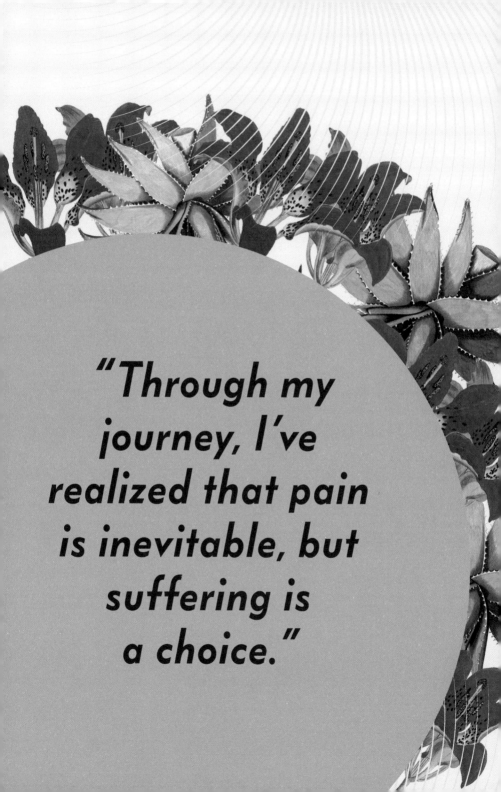

"Through my journey, I've realized that pain is inevitable, but suffering is a choice."

Her experience in Florida would eventually lead her to found *TransTech Social Enterprise*, a web development academy and graphic design firm that offers apprenticeships to trans people with drive but limited skills. "It's one of the only sectors where a trans person can do business remotely, meaning we'll be more likely to be judged on the quality of our work rather than our gender identity. It's a lifeboat for people who are drowning," she said. "My life has not been an easy one, and yet to have survived what I've survived and to still have love in my heart is a gift. To be a trans woman of color and even live to see 34 is a gift. Through my journey, I've realized that pain is inevitable, but suffering is a choice."

Pouring Into Her Community

Once upon a time, Angelica was fighting to survive, now she's fighting for so much more. Through her advocacy and immersive leadership, she's been able to create work opportunities for trans people all across America. Whether in the boardroom, on the set of a movie, or on Capitol Hill, Angelica Ross is a driving force for racial and transgender equality. In 2020, Angelica became a face of Nicolas Ghesquière's pre-Fall campaign for Louis Vuitton; a campy homage to vintage sci-fi book covers. Her acting breakthrough came in the form of Ryan Murphy's Award Winning FX hit, *Pose*—which follows NYC's Black and Latino LGBTQ and gender-nonconforming ballroom culture scene, in the '80s and early '90s. The show made history by featuring the largest transgender cast for a scripted series. She's appeared in various mediums, including television, film, and theater, and has even worked behind the camera as an executive producer. Through it all, she's learned that helping people recognize their value is her true calling.

Activism and
Social Justice

Darnella Frazier

Fighting for justice and equality

On May 25, 2020, Darnella Frazier's life changed forever. Her nine-year-old cousin wanted snacks, so the pair walked to a neighboring grocery store. However, Darnella never made it inside. Before she could enter the store, she witnessed George Floyd being wrestled to the ground by police officers. She told her cousin to go into the store without her, and quickly began filming the interaction on her phone. Moments after hitting record, she heard George tell the police he couldn't breathe. Darnella was horrified. For eight minutes and forty-eight seconds, she watched Derek Chauvin kneel on George's neck. In his final moments, he begged them not to kill him and called out for his mother. Darnella heard all of it.

On May 26, at 1:46 am, she posted the video on Facebook with the caption: "They killed him right in front of cup foods over south on 38th and Chicago!! No type of sympathy </3 </3 #POLICEBRUTALITY." The video went viral.

"I opened my phone and I started recording because I knew if I didn't, no one would believe me," said Darnella in a statement released by her attorney. When the Minneapolis Police Department issued a misleading statement about Floyd's death, called "Man Dies After Medical Incident During Police Interaction," Darnella was not having it. She responded saying, "Medical incident??? Watch outtt they killed him and the proof is clearlyyyy there!!"

"I opened my phone and I started recording because I knew if I didn't, no one would believe me."

The next day, she returned to the murder scene and was immediately embraced by protestors asking her how she felt. She didn't know how to respond. "I don't know how to feel, cause it's so sad, bro. This man was literally right here at 8:00 pm yesterday. I was walking my cousin to the store, and I just see him on the ground and I'm like 'What is going on?'" She was traumatized, but her bravery would be the catalyst that mobilized people into action. For weeks after that fateful day, she was unable to sleep. The unwanted publicity forced her to leave her home and move around from hotel to hotel. Then there was the anxiety that came every time she saw a police car.

Justice for George Floyd

On the one-year anniversary of George's death, Darnella released a statement speaking publicly about her trauma from witnessing his murder, and how she knew her life could never be the same. She criticized the over-policing and racial profiling of Black communities, and its long-term effects on her own mental health. "These officers shouldn't get to decide if someone gets to live or not. It's time these officers start getting held accountable. Murdering people and abusing your power while doing it is not doing your job."

Then, there was the overwhelming feeling of helplessness; she couldn't save him that day. All she could do was record his final moments. She concluded by speaking directly to Floyd: "I can't express enough how I wish things could have went different, but I want you to know you will always be in my heart. I'll always remember this day because of you. May your soul rest in peace. May you rest in the most beautiful roses."

When Derek Chauvin was first convicted, legal analysts agreed that Darnella's video would play a key role in dismantling the misleading statements being peddled by police. They were right. During the trial, Darnella's video was one of the most important pieces of evidence used to sentence Chauvin. In her testimony, she said, "It's been nights I stayed up apologizing and apologizing to George Floyd for not doing more and not physically interacting and not saving his life." She also testified that "When I look at George Floyd, I look at my dad, I look at my brothers, I look at my cousins, my uncles, because they're all Black. I have a Black father. I have a Black brother. I have Black friends," adding, "I look at how that could have been them."

"These officers shouldn't get to decide if someone gets to live or not. It's time these officers start getting held accountable."

Although Derek Chauvin was found guilty, was justice really served? George Floyd's family will never be the same, and neither will Darnella's. This is the unspoken trauma of racism. Even when the law decides in our favor, we are still at a loss because we are forced to live with the emotional scars. But we continue to do this work, of fighting for justice and equality because we have to.

Sônia Guajajara

Fighting against anonymity

Sônia Guajajara has always been an activist. Born to a Guajajara family on Araribóia Indigenous Land in the Amazonian rainforest, she left home at 15 after an invitation from the National Indian Foundation, encouraging her to attend a boarding school focused on agricultural education. She later attended the Federal University of Maranhão, located in the state capital of São Luís, and went on to obtain a master's degree in culture and society from the Institute of Humanities, Arts, and Culture at the Federal University of Bahia. Sônia has worked in a variety of professions, including as a teacher and a nurse, but her calling has always been protecting the rights and freedoms of her people.

"I've spent my whole life fighting against anonymity, against indigenous peoples' invisibility," she said. "I always wanted to find a path, a way to bring the history and way of life of the indigenous people to light for society as a whole." Currently, she is the leader of the Articulation of the Indigenous Peoples of Brazil, an organization that represents around 300 Indigenous ethnic groups in Brazil.

"We Exist"

As an Indigenous woman, Sônia is familiar with the feeling of being erased from movements and from her homeland. In many Eurocentric cultures, land that is "untouched" is seen as a raw resource that is free for the taking. This viewpoint ultimately ignores traditional ways of living and effectively erases Indigenous land usage and presence. For Sônia, her community, and many Indigenous groups around the world, the human relationship with land is meant to be rooted in preservation, not consumption.

"The essence of Indigenous peoples is collectivity, and a respectful relationship with nature and with ancestry," she said. "In general, those who do not descend from Indians cannot see nature as part of themselves. People want to create and change landscapes and develop a very close relationship with consumption. They need to have more cars, lots of trendy clothes, a good job and status. Individual identity is everything. The lack of a collective identity leaves a void in their lives."

She sees that this void and need for consumption drives people away from their own inner knowing, and toward self-destructive behaviors. "In the city, even if residents complain about pollution, they continue polluting. They complain about the traffic, but they do not stop buying cars. They work all the time to satisfy the individual, to the detriment of the collective," she said. "In contrast, for the Indigenous, it is the collective spirit that prevails. We fight for land, but no one struggles to have a piece of land for himself."

Preserving Life

For Sônia, protecting land is about protecting her people and her way of life. "When you destroy nature and foreclose the indigenous peoples' way of life, preventing them from exercising their culture, you are killing them. If we do not follow our culture, our tradition, we are no longer people," she said. She's been threatened, attacked, and government officials in Brazil have repeatedly tried to silence her, yet through it all she has continued her fight for the rights of her people and the Indigenous way of life.

"Indigenous Peoples have suffered from historical processes of prejudice and racism that for a long time delegitimized our voice in the public sphere," she said. "However, with a lot of struggle, we have been changing this reality. There is still a lot to achieve and spaces to occupy."

> *"My mission is to make the larger society see the huge potential of indigenous people to help preserve life."*

Her purpose has always been bigger than her. It's also always been bigger than her community. "My mission is to make the larger society see the huge potential of indigenous people to help preserve life," she said. "And how our way of life naturally acts as a barrier against chaos. The world needs us badly, because the way we live and act can help avert this wave of disaster and destruction that is approaching."

In addition to grassroots work, Sônia has also emphasized the importance of having government representation. In 2018, she announced her intention to run for President of Brazil, and had her candidacy supported by the ecosocialist wing of the party. Ultimately, she ended up being chosen by the labor leader Guilherme Boulos to serve as his vice presidential running mate and became the first Indigenous person to run for a federal executive office in Brazil.

Dolores Huerta

A living civil rights icon

Dolores Clara Fernández Huerta was born in a small mining community in the mountain range of northern New Mexico. Political and community activism were deeply rooted in her upbringing; her father, Juan Fernández, was a farm worker, miner, and early union activist who ran for political office in the New Mexico legislature in 1938. Her mother, Alicia, was an active community member with a fiery independence and a distinct entrepreneurial spirit. As a hotel owner, she was known for her compassion and kindness to others and regularly welcomed low-wage workers into her 70-room hotel, often waiving fees for those who could not afford it. These early examples of community-rooted social justice were pillars in Dolores's future work.

Credit Where Credit Is Due

She is a living civil rights icon, and yet most of her work has long been overshadowed by that of Cesar Chavez, her long-time collaborator, and the cofounder of what would eventually become known as the United Farm Workers of America union. Even her famous battle cry, "Sí se puede"—Spanish for "Yes, we can"—is most commonly attributed to Obama's 2008 campaign. It's a common story; some women create movements out of love, that are then co-opted by someone more favored by society. History is rewritten, and we lose our heroes. Dolores is a testament to the importance of writing our stories and telling the truth.

It began when Dolores was a teenager. She was outraged by the numerous economic and racial injustices that she saw in California's agricultural Central Valley. At 25, she became the political director of the Community Service Organization, run by influential community organizer Fred Ross.

There she met Cesar and in 1962 the two teamed up to form the United Farm Workers, to fight for the rights of farmworkers who often toiled for wages as low as 70 cents an hour in inhumane conditions. These workers often didn't have access to bathrooms, rest periods, or clean drinking water. In 1965, Dolores led farmworkers on a strike and experienced overwhelming violence and sexism on the picket lines. Surprisingly, or perhaps unsurprisingly, the violence came from both fronts—those she was fighting for and those she was fighting against.

One of her children said the movement was her "most important child."

Nevertheless, she persisted. The movement was bigger than any opposing voices. It was also bigger than her. Although lawmakers began referring to Dolores as Cesar's sidekick, she knew it was just a distraction. She was unconventional in every sense of the word. As a twice divorced single mother to 11 children, she knew the opposition would do everything possible to discredit and invalidate the necessary work she was carrying out. "Who supports those kids when she's out on these adventures?" one of her opponents is shown asking in historical footage. What's remarkable about Dolores's leadership is her ability to detach ego from the work.

The Revolution

The movement took everything from her, and although history books tried to erase her, her legacy lives on. In a recent documentary on Dolores's life, her children spoke openly about the love and admiration they had for her. But it was also clear how much the revolution took from them. One of her children said the movement was her "most important child."

> "We do need women to ... be in political office. We need a feminist to be at the table when decisions are being made."

"I think that's something that all mothers have to deal with, especially single mothers. We work and we have to leave the kids behind. And I think that's one of the reasons that we, not only as women but as families, we have to advocate for early childhood education for all of our children," she said.

"To make sure that they're taken care of but also educated in the process. Because we do need women in civic life. We do need women to run for office, to be in political office. We need a feminist to be at the table when decisions are being made so that the right decisions will be made."

Malala Yousafzai

A fighter and survivor

It started with a blog when Malala Yousafzai was just eleven years old. Using the pen name "Gul Makai," Malala began to write about her desire to learn and go to school. She described being forced to stay home and questioned the intentions of the Taliban. In a blog post titled "I am Afraid," she wrote about her nightmares and the fears she had about a full-blown war in her hometown, Swat Valley.

In 2009, those fears came true, violence in her hometown forced Malala and her family to evacuate. It would be weeks before Malala could return. When she did, she committed to being even louder about what she and other young girls were experiencing under the Taliban's regime. As her audience and influence grew, the Taliban began to take notice. In 2011, she was nominated for the International Children's Peace Prize. That same year, she was awarded Pakistan's National Youth Peace Prize.

Then on the morning of October 9, 2012, 15-year-old Malala was shot by the Taliban.

The Cost of Being Brave

She was on the bus and heading home from school when it happened. Deeply engaged in conversation with her friends, she didn't notice the bus come to a halting stop. A young man boarded the bus and asked for Malala by name. When she came forward, he fired three shots at her, causing critical injuries. She was rushed to a hospital in Peshawar and four days later she was airlifted to an intensive care unit in England. Although she would require multiple surgeries, including repair of a facial nerve to fix the paralyzed left side of her face, she had suffered no major brain damage. After weeks of treatment and therapy, Malala was able to begin attending school in Birmingham, only this time, her audience wasn't limited to those who read her anonymous blog; she had captured the attention of the world. This was just the beginning.

"We realize the importance of our voices only when we are silenced."

Protests erupted around the world, and her name began to symbolize a new wave of global feminism. The UN special envoy for global education introduced a petition that called for all children around the world to be back in school by 2015. That petition birthed the ratification of Pakistan's first Right to Education bill. "We realize the importance of our voices only when we are silenced," said Malala. "Once I had asked God for one or two extra inches in height, but instead he made me as tall as the sky, so high that I could not measure myself."

Stepping Into Power

Malala's first public appearance after the shooting was her 16th birthday in 2013, when she addressed 500 people at the United Nations in New York City. After her speech, Secretary-General

Ban Ki-moon pronounced July 12, Yousafzai's birthday, "Malala Day" in honor of the young leader's activism.

That same year, she was named as one of *Time* magazine's most influential people and awarded the United Nations Human Rights Prize. She also coauthored her memoir, *I Am Malala: The Girl Who Stood Up for Education and Was Shot by the Taliban*. She later became the youngest person to win the Liberty Medal, awarded by the National Constitution Center in Philadelphia to public figures striving for people's freedom throughout the world. Nominated for the Nobel Peace Prize in 2013 but passed over that year, Yousafzai won the prize in 2014, becoming the youngest Nobel Laureate.

In congratulating Yousafzai, Pakistani Prime Minister Nawaz Sharif said: "She is (the) pride of Pakistan, she has made her countrymen proud. Her achievement is unparalleled and unequaled. Girls and boys of the world should take lead from her struggle and commitment." Former U.N. Secretary-General Ban Ki-moon described Yousafzai as "a brave and gentle advocate of peace who, through the simple act of going to school, became a global teacher." In April 2017, United Nations Secretary-General Antonio Guterres appointed Yousafzai as a U.N. Messenger of Peace to promote girls' education. The appointment is the highest honor given by the United Nations, for an initial period of two years. Today Malala's fund continues to work for a world where every girl can learn and lead.

In her autobiography, Malala asked, "If one man can destroy everything, why can't one girl change it?" She has spent the majority of her life being that one girl, to change it all.

Dr. Alaa Murabit

A women's rights advocate

As a Muslim woman, born in Canada and raised equally between the Saskatchewan prairies and her ancestral homeland in Libya, Dr. Alaa Murabit saw firsthand the power of investing in grassroots initiatives. She found her calling during the Arab Spring. It was the winter of 2011 and Tunisia had erupted in protest, which soon spread to Egypt, Yemen, Syria, Bahrain, and Libya. The world watched as regimes collapsed because the people demanded change. It was a powerful demonstration of what could happen when the collective came together. For 42 years, the late Mummar Gaddafi had ruled over Libya, but on February 17th, 2011, the Libyan people took to the streets and demanded an end to his regime. As the calls for radical change amplified, Libyan society shifted and women began assuming prominent leadership roles within the revolution, bringing gender-based issues to the forefront. But as the months went on, and the revolution began to stabilize, Alaa noticed a troubling trend: the women who had braved the front lines and gave their voices to a movement were being pushed aside. She knew she needed to act.

Becoming the Voice

In response, she founded Voice of Libyan Women, an advocacy group focused on the political participation and economic empowerment of Libyan women. Months of protesting on the frontlines had given Libyan women a taste of social involvement that had long been denied to them through cultural barriers and expectations. What Alaa realized was that there were thousands of Libyan women just like her, who were ready and desperate to speak up. What they needed was a collective that would stand by them always. She decided to build an organization that could do just that.

Soon, mosques, coffee shops ... were having conversations that would have been considered taboo just months earlier.

Within months of organizing, Voice of Libyan Women put together their first-ever International Women's Conference in Libya. At the time, Alaa was a final-year medical student. Shortly after, they launched Project Noor, a program that sought to end the stigma on domestic violence and sexual abuse. Through social media campaigns and traditional press, the project brought difficult conversations to the forefront of Libyan society. The response to the campaign was overwhelming. Soon, mosques, coffee shops, and community centers were having conversations that would have been considered taboo just months earlier. By rooting the campaign in religious texts, the organization was able to push back on cultural beliefs that normalized turning a blind eye to gender-based violence. Soon, neighboring nations began reaching out to Voice of Libyan Women for support in organizing similar campaigns. Nearly a decade after the agency launched, the organization has expanded its reach, with a focus on women's empowerment, development and growth through practical on-the-ground measures, legal advocacy, and community engagement, and has amassed 600 volunteers.

From Libya to the World

Mobilizing women in her homeland inspired Alaa to take her politics and advocacy work to the global stage. Equipped with a medical degree and her Masters in International Strategy and Diplomacy from the London School of Economics, she began to work closely with the United Nations as a consultant. In 2015, she became a member of the High-Level Advisory Group for the Global Study on the Implementation of Security Resolution 1325, commissioned by the UN Secretary-General. The study emphasized the importance between the involvement of women in politics and stability in a region.

Today Alaa is recognized as one of the leading global health and inclusive security experts of her generation and is currently serving the United Nations on the High-Level Commission on Health Employment & Economic Growth. In addition to her work with the UN, Alaa also serves as a board member for the Malala Fund, and has been named a Harvard Radcliffe Fellow, MIT Media Lab Director's Fellow, and Ashoka Fellow. In 2018, she was presented with the Nelson Mandela International Change-Maker Award by the Nelson Mandela Family, and was listed one of the 2019 Top 20 Most Influential People in Gender Equality Policy in the world alongside Ruth Bader Ginsburg, Angela Merkel, and Michelle Obama.

What makes Alaa's work impactful is her commitment to creating programs that embrace the cultural nuances of communities. By creating programs that tackled women's issues from the perspective of a person living in Libya, she was able to have purpose-driven conversations. This is often not the case with development work. A one-size-fits-all solution is given without understanding the people's needs. By applying a people-first approach, Alaa's work has redesigned global approaches to gender equity and is changing how many organizations see development work.

Dr. Sima Samar

A courageous human rights defender

One year after the beginning of the communist revolution in Afghanistan, Sima Samar's life was forever changed. It was 1978, and the Soviet-backed coup was unfolding in Afghanistan. In the dead of the night, ten men broke into her home, kidnapping her husband and his three brothers. She never saw them again. Slowly, people around Sima began disappearing, as if they were being erased off the face of the earth. To this day, what happened to them remains a mystery, but the heaviness of not knowing soon became the norm. During that long and dreadful period, Sima lost 60 members of her family through similar disappearances. Homes in her neighborhood sat empty, and the women in her circles told similar stories of sudden arrests and the unspoken ghosts among them. The air was saturated with fear, and the salt of tearful nights. While the women around her quietly ruminated over what would become of them, Sima knew she was being called to step into what had always been her life path.

Born a Feminist

Samar found her voice in the seventh grade. Between growing up with ten brothers and sisters in a polygamist household, and the cultural burdens of being a girl, she saw how gender inequity penetrated every aspect of daily life. Her personal experiences as a

Hazara, an ethnic minority in Afghanistan, also allowed her to see how class, lineage, and gender could dictate a person's experiences. It was these early experiences that created the backbone of her life trajectory and shaped her into the fearless advocate she is today.

From an early age, she knew that she needed to pursue higher education to make the changes she so desperately wanted to see. But her father had other plans. He wanted her to get married, and follow the traditions laid out before her. Skillfully, they reached a compromise —she would agree to an arranged marriage, but only if she would also be allowed to attend university. It was on this condition that she married her late husband, Abdul Chafoor Sultani, who promised her that she would be able to go to medical school.

In 1982, four years after her husband was kidnapped, she started her studies. Samara graduated from Kabul University and became the first Hazara woman in Afghanistan to receive a medical degree. She began her career practicing medicine at a government hospital in Kabul, but that was short-lived. It was becoming too dangerous to continue living in Afghanistan, and Samra had the safety and well-being of her young son to worry about. Tearfully, she left the job she had worked so hard for and said goodbye to Kabul. Like many of her fellow countrymen, she sought refuge in neighboring Pakistan. Fortunately, she was able to continue working as a doctor at the refugee branch of Mission Hospital. It was there, in the underfunded and makeshift facilities, that she was reminded again of her calling.

The Fight for Equality

Since the late 1970s, women and girls in Afghanistan have been denied the most basic human rights under the guise of religion and culture. For women like Sima, it was clear that this oppression wasn't rooted in any dogma, it was the invention of a patriarchal system and she could not allow it to continue. While working at refugee hospitals in Pakistan she decided to start her own hospital, catering specifically to the needs of Afghan women and children in Quetta.

By 1989, her single refugee hospital had grown into the Shuhada Organization and expanded beyond health care. The organization began offering training programs for aspiring nurses, community health workers and traditional birth attendants. It also began offering reproductive health education clinics. From 1989-2011, the organization benefited over 3.3 million people. What started as a clinic grew into an empowering movement. By 2012, the Shuhada Organization operated 71 schools in Afghanistan and 34 schools in Pakistan for Afghan refugees. During the Taliban's regime, Shuhada schools were among the few schools that accepted girls. Sima's love for education, female empowerment, and her country gave her the courage to risk her life every single day. In 2001, she returned to her homeland and began her term as the Deputy Chair and Minister of Women's Affairs for the Interim Administration of Afghanistan. She was one of only two women cabinet ministers in the transition government and went on to establish the first-ever Ministry of Women's Affairs in the country. Under her brave leadership, the ministry restored the rights of women and improved their political, economic, legal, and social status.

Under her brave leadership, the ministry went on to restore the rights of women.

With the Taliban's return in 2021, Afghanistan's future is unclear. What we do know is that women like Sima have dedicated their lives to empowering women to demand equal justice. Her valiant efforts have contributed to educating a nation, and inspiring generations to be the change.

Film and Television

Michaela Coel

Never doubt your intuition

When Michaela Coel first pitched *I May Destroy You* to Netflix in 2017, she was offered $1 million for full rights to the 12-episode series. But she turned it down. Yes, it was a generous sum; however, there were strings attached to the offer that caused her to pause and ask pivotal questions.

During a phone conversation with a Netflix executive, Michaela remembers asking for 5 percent of the copyright. Retaining some ownership would allow her to earn royalties and have rights to her creative production, but she quickly learned that wasn't an option. "There was just silence on the phone," Michaela recalled. "The executive said, 'It's not how we do things here. Nobody does that, it's not a big deal.'" She thought to herself, if it wasn't a big deal, then why were they making it one? However, the streaming service didn't budge and neither did she.

This project was much more than a paycheck for the award-winning actor and producer; this was her story and she wanted ownership rights. "I remember thinking, I've been going down rabbit holes in my head, like people thinking I'm paranoid, I'm acting sketchy, I'm killing off all my agents," Michaela said. There were naysayers; many of the people around her pushed back on her decision and tried to change her mind. But when she found out that her agents were set to receive an undisclosed amount of money from Netflix if she took the offer, she knew walking away was in her best interest. She rejected the $1 million dollar offer, distanced herself from those who doubted her intuition and fired her agents. For Michaela, the lesson here was clear—she was an artist, and her art was to be created and shared on her terms.

Finding Her Footing and Living Her Art

Michaela-Moses Ewuraba O Boakye-Collinson was born in London, to two Ghanaian parents. She grew up in East London and was raised predominantly by her mother, a devout Pentecostal Christian.

She first began receiving international recognition in 2015 with the release of her breakout series, *Chewing Gum*. The show was a perfect cocktail of awkward British humor and universal Black girl experiences. It was real. The characters were largely based on people or experiences that Coel had grown up with in government housing. *Chewing Gum* was one of the rare shows that indirectly challenged the many stereotypes about low-income families, by introducing the audience to colorful characters who, while flawed, were also deeply lovable.

It wasn't an aspirational story of escaping poverty. Instead, it was very much grounded in the reality of everyday life. With the release of *I May Destroy You*, and her brave decision to reject the purchase offer from Netflix, it's clear that as a creative and a business owner, Coel is loyal to her talents and the experiences that shaped her.

But that wasn't always the case. Her first series went through 41 drafts before it aired. The first version was a 20-minute one-woman play

She was an artist, and her art was to be created and shared on her terms.

during Michaela's last year at Guildhall School of Music and Drama in London. She decided to remove herself from the school's big year-end show after realizing she was trying to be someone she wasn't.

The show, the school, and so many of the experiences she had longed for could never make her happy, because they weren't her. Instead of going along with the show, she decided to tell her own story. From that realization, the version of *Chewing Gum* that so many bonded over was born.

On Self-Advocacy, and Building Your Career

In 2017, *I May Destroy You* was picked up by the BBC, with HBO as a coproducer and Michaela maintaining ownership rights. Her determination paid off tenfold. The series won the BAFTAs for Best Mini-Series, Best Director: Drama, Best Writer: Drama, and Best Actress, in addition to two RTS Programme Awards, two Independent Spirit Awards, a Gotham Award, a GLAAD Media Award, an NAACP Image Award, and a Peabody Award. It was the most critically acclaimed TV show of 2020 and Michaela was just getting started.

The success of I May Destroy You served as a reminder for her; anything is possible when you are authentic to your voice and honor your boundaries.

The success of *I May Destroy You* served as a reminder for her; anything is possible when you are authentic to your voice and honor your boundaries. History is laced with the forgotten stories of creatives who've been in Michaela's position. In many instances, companies can manipulate and distort those who are hoping to break into a competitive market and those who do not have industry ties. It's not that Michaela necessarily knew better or had reason to be skeptical of the offer. What makes her a creative to watch, both on and off the screen, is her reluctance to settle for the status quo and her diligent commitment to her authenticity. She believed in herself in abundance.

Think of the shows that you are really drawn to. The ones that pull at your heartstrings and keep you up at night rewriting endings or grieving the loss of your favorite character. What do they have in common? It could be that you related to the storyline, or that you deeply connected with one of the characters, but there's more to it than that. As human beings, we are drawn to stories that make us feel. Whether it's fear, anger, melancholy, or suspense, good television, good books, and good music have the power to connect you to yourself. This is Michaela's single greatest skill. She has the uncanny ability to take her everyday life, from the mundane and ordinary, to the trauma many of us keep hidden, and turn it into powerful art.

Whatever project she chooses to release next, what we know for sure is that it will be layered with pieces of her story and those around her. As she lives her life authentically out loud, she gives each of us permission to do the same.

Ava
DuVernay

Directing her own path

Ava DuVernay is a celebrated director, producer, and screenwriter, who has created powerful works of art including *Selma*, *When They See Us*, *A Wrinkle in Time*, *13th*, and *Queen Sugar*. Her films have captivated and inspired generations, earning her countless accolades and solidifying her name in history. However, her journey into the industry has been far from traditional. "I didn't have that NYU, Spike Lee experience," she shared with *Hello Sunshine*. Instead, she majored in English literature and African American studies at the University of California, Los Angeles. It was there that she decided she was interested in pursuing a career in broadcast journalism.

Her talents quickly earned her a coveted internship with CBS News, and that's where things began to change. Rather than solidifying her career interests, the internship pointed her elsewhere.

"I was working on the national evening news with Connie Chung and Dan Rather during the O.J. Simpson trial. I was one of 10 interns who were dispatched to cover a juror," recalled Ava in an interview with *UCLA Magazine*. "I was to sit outside the juror's house, look through trash, and do all the things I thought were not becoming of a broadcast journalist." The case was a turning point in the crossover between hard news and celebrity gossip columns and became a clear indicator that traditional journalism was not Ava's calling. She quickly pivoted into film marketing and publicity, and in 1999 she launched her own publicity firm called The DuVernay Agency, where she worked with films like *Collateral, Dream Girls*, and *Invictus*. It would be years before she picked up a camera.

"I knew that as a black woman in this industry, I wouldn't have people knocking down my door to give me money for my projects."

Coming Into Her Purpose

Filmmaking was never part of her plan. Even though she directed her first documentary in 2008, it wasn't until 2010 that she realized there were stories she needed to tell. On a $50,000 budget, she shot and directed her first feature film, *I Will Follow*, in 11 days. Her storytelling captivated filmgoers and critics alike. The independent drama told the raw story of a grieving woman and the 12 visitors who helped her move forward into a new world. According to critic Roger Ebert, it was one of the best films he'd ever seen about the loss of a loved one.

Ava had found her calling. As she started to come into her talents, she began taking private directing classes while maintaining her day job. "I kept my publicity job while making my first three films," she said to CNBC. "I knew that as a black woman in this industry, I wouldn't have people knocking down my door to give me money for my projects, so I was happy to make them on the side while working my day job."

Ava's second feature film, *Middle of Nowhere*, was a testament to the range of her storytelling. When asked about what inspired the film, she said that although the film was not personal, it was built around common elements in the Black and Brown communities she was familiar with. "Mother, daughters, sisters, and wives—it's certainly something I've observed, a secret society of all these women waiting and we never see or hear their stories," she said in *Entropy Magazine*. "I was always kind of interested in that. At one point I thought I might just do a documentary but then I started coming up with the story of Ruby and Derek and really playing with this idea of how they're separated and why. It's not personal directly, but definitely important to me and the part of the community that I want to project." The film premiered at the 2012 *Sundance Film Festival* and won the award for Best Direction.

Shortly after, her career took off and she steadily became a household name. She built her repertoire by directing TV shows, commercials, and even music videos. In 2014, DuVernay became the first Black woman to be nominated for a Golden Globe Award for Best Director for her work on *Selma*—a feature film about Martin Luther King, Jr.'s campaign to secure equal voting rights.

Honoring Your Path

Nearly 15 years after picking up a camera for the first time, Ava directed the video for rapper and business mogul Jay Z's song "Family Feud," which became the cultural event of 2017. "For me to pick up a camera as a black woman who did not go to film school—this is a testament to whatever path you're on right now is not necessarily the path you have to stay on," Ava told *Refinery29*. "If you're on a path that's not the one that you want to be on, you can

> *DuVernay became the first Black woman to be nominated for a Golden Globe Award*

also pivot, and you can also move, and age doesn't make a difference, race, gender. It's about putting one step in front of another, about forward movement to where you wanna be."

Her advice to aspiring filmmakers, or to anyone who desires a career shift, is simple, "You have to go in and in the back of your mind the subtext is 'I am the one.' Don't be afraid to do the small jobs. Nothing is beneath you."

Ava did not walk a linear path. However, even with the odds stacked against her in a highly saturated and competitive market, she chose to believe that she was capable and that she would find a way. "When people tell [my story], it's about race and gender—'black woman director'—but my story's also really about age, because I didn't pick up a camera until I was 32," said Ava, in an interview with *Refinery29*. All she had was what was inside of her, and the unwavering belief that she was enough. When we expect perfection, and deny ourselves permission to learn and grow, we are subconsciously setting ourselves up for failure.

It's never too late to change your mind and go after the things that bring you joy. It's okay to grow and evolve past the life you thought you wanted. You just need to be brave enough to try.

"When people tell [my story], it's about race and gender—'black woman director'—but my story's also really about age, because I didn't pick up a camera until I was 32."

Issa
Rae

Telling your story

Standing on the red carpet at the 2017 Emmy Awards, Issa Rae was asked who she was rooting for. Her response unintentionally became a generational anthem—she was rooting for everyone Black. While the moment may have been candid, it was undeniably on brand for the multihyphenate creative. Bold, honest, and seamlessly encompassing; Issa has always bet on Black.

That includes betting on the strength of her own vision and story. In less than a decade, Rae has been a two-time Golden Globe nominee, Primetime Emmy Awards nominee, *New York Times* bestselling author, and counting. And this self-described Awkward Black Girl shows no signs of slowing down. Looking ahead, she's developing multiple movies and shows, in addition to co-owning two coffee shops, a hair-care brand, and starting her own production company.

Making Your Dreams Work for You

Before the awards and the acclaim, Rae was an African Studies and Political Studies student at Stanford University. A longtime comedy fan, she noticed that many of the series she loved to unwind with had all-white casts and weren't reflective of her experiences. But she also remembered a time when it was different.

The young creator grew up watching sitcoms like *Moesha*, *Girlfriends*, *Living Single*, and *A Different World*, where Black characters were multifaceted and in leading roles. This was an era where almost every night of the week, an all-Black cast could be found on major networks. But then, the landscape of television began to change. Although *Living Single* preceded *Friends*, the latter quickly gained exponential popularity across diverse demographics, in spite of an all-white cast. Production companies saw this as a sign—maybe diversity didn't matter. At the same time, *Living Single* started to suffer in the ongoing ratings battle against bigger shows. As a result, networks pivoted away from the all-Black casts of the '90s and thus began the end of Black sitcoms. Instead, Rae felt people of color were increasingly only shown as stereotypes or archetypes in the more "relatable" stories of white characters. As she once said, "So much of the media now presents Blackness as being cool, or able to dance, or fierce and flawless, or just out of control; I'm not any of those things."

"I got really frustrated and just wanted to start making my own stories."

So what did Rae do? Equipped with a camera and a few friends, she produced *Dream Diaries*, a mock-reality show, featuring an all-Black cast and formatted in the style of MTV's *The Real World*. Without much thought and without a blueprint, she shared the production on social media and the internet took over. It quickly circulated beyond her circle and reached an audience far outside the walls of her college. Rae was onto something. She had tapped into a niche many hadn't seen on television before—everyday Blackness. But for Rae, it wasn't about finding a niche so much as it was about being herself.

Bloom Where You Are Planted

Long before becoming the media maven she is today, Rae was the Awkward Black Girl without a blueprint. Born in Los Angeles to a Senegalese father and mother from Louisiana, Rae has spent much of her life straddling drastically different worlds. During her early years, her family temporarily relocated to Senegal, before settling in a predominantly white neighborhood in Maryland. There she says she "grew up with things that aren't considered 'Black,' like the swim team and street hockey and Passover dinners with Jewish best friends." Then her family moved back to Los Angeles, where she attended a predominantly Black middle school. Overnight, she went from being the Black girl to not-Black-enough. Many of the cultural growing pains that Rae experienced became the stories and cringe-worthy moments featured in her creative productions. In-between-ness became her signature—the essence of what is so loved by fans of *Awkward Black Girl* and *Insecure*.

Rae's lived experience has given her the power to create characters that are familiar to so many Black women. Issa, Molly, Lawrence, and many more of Rae's characters, each represent a dynamic part of the Black experience. When Rae created *Awkward Black Girl*, she was entering that uncomfortable post-grad-what-happens-next season of life—the quarter life crisis so many of us try to ignore. Instead of ignoring what was going on inside of her, Rae decided to make art. While she had previously created scripted content for YouTube, the reaction to *Awkward Black Girl* was different. "I remember uploading it and just being terrified of the feedback because I was putting myself out there on the internet in a new way," Rae recalls. "After spending all night editing it, I thought f**k it and uploaded the first episode—I woke up to so much positivity." Ten years later, the first episode has nearly 3 million views.

Say It Loud, I'm Black and I'm Proud

Rae's commitment to telling her own story on her own terms has continuously allowed her to dominate on the big screen, in the producer's chair, and in the writer's room. It's what makes her Issa Rae. "Sometimes the white writers will be like, 'I didn't even know what that line meant until I watched the show,' and I'm like, 'That's OK. There are some things that are just for us.'" *Insecure* is made for Black people by Black people, but it's also a show that wryly educates white people. No matter what angle you approach it from, it forces you to reflect on your own behavior and biases.

"People constantly make excuses on why they can't follow their dreams. Stop finding the ways that you can't and start finding the ways that you can."

Every celebration and every setback has come with lessons, and Rae has paid close attention and taken notes. Although her early webseries didn't go viral, the project taught her the importance of consistency and the power of creating opportunities. It also gave her the platform to launch her breakthrough series, *Awkward Black Girl*, catapulting her career trajectory and building a fanbase. Perhaps it's the inbetweenness that's defined so much of her life, or the committed refusal to be put into a box that's devoted Rae to a lifetime of creating spaces reflective of her, and inclusive of all sides of Black culture. Whatever the reason, the culture is grateful and thriving as a result.

Standing in Purpose and Truth

Rae knew early on that her purpose was beyond diversifying Hollywood; she's here to create content where Blackness is the norm, not the focal point. To date, her work has seldom, if ever, waivered from that purpose. "My definition of Blackness on screen and how I choose to reflect it is in the most grounded way. I've always made it clear that my characters are very specific Black people—I'm not trying to represent an entire race with my work because I can't do that and it's not my place to do so."

But what she does do, and consistently, is commit to her purpose. When she started writing the pilot for *Insecure*, she knew it was not going to be a political show. Blackness was the root, but there were nuances. "I just wanted to see my friends and I reflected on television, in the same way that white people are allowed, and which nobody questions," continues Rae. By sticking to her calling Rae delivered a series that is being called revolutionary. But for her, it's just regular life. "I'm not burdened by the racial strife of it all. They can just be two people falling in love or solving a crime. The statement that I want to make at the end of the day is just existing."

As she closes the door on *Insecure*, and leaves behind the 30-something year old version of herself, she is doing what Issa has always done and blooming where she is planted. Recently, the icon

> *"I just want to do my pure story, and if I'm not, it's just not worth it."*

renewed a five-year production deal with HBO & Warner and has shown no signs of slowing down. For some, *Insecure* could have been the pinnacle of their career and they could have coasted on its success. There's no doubt that Rae could have written a ten-season series, but that wouldn't be her. Instead, she is sticking to her internal storyline and honoring her growth.

Lena
Waithe

Differences are our superpowers

In 2017, Lena Waithe made history when she became the first Black American woman to win the Primetime Emmy Award for Outstanding Writing for a Comedy Series. "Here's the irony of it all," she said in an interview with *Vanity Fair*. "I don't need an Emmy to tell me to go to work. I've been working. I've been writing, I've been developing, I've been putting pieces together and I'm bullets, you know what I'm saying?"

Taking Chances

When Lena arrived in Hollywood in 2016, she had no family, no friends, and no money. She began her career as an assistant to director Gina Prince-Bythewood, of *Love & Basketball*. Soon after, she became a production assistant on Ava DuVernay's scripted directorial debut, *I Will Follow*. Although she wasn't writing scripts like she intended, the people around her were taking notice. She eventually became a writer for the Fox Television series *Bones* and the 2012 Nickelodeon sitcom *How to Rock*, and a producer for the 2014 satirical comedy film *Dear White People*. While these shows added to her portfolio and gave her industry credentials, it was the original content she produced that truly shone a light on her undeniable talent and bolstered her influence. In 2014, *Variety* named Lena one of its "10 Comedians to Watch" and in August 2015, Showtime commissioned a pilot for an original series, written by Lena and produced by Common. *The Chi* tells a young Black American man's coming-of-age story. For Lena, this story was intertwined with her own. In writing the scripts, she intentionally chose to salvage her own experiences growing up on the South Side of Chicago, and craft stories that painted a more nuanced portrait of the people and communities she intimately knew.

Then in 2015, she gained the role that would afford her an Emmy and the recognition she always deserved. She was cast in the Netflix series *Master of None* after meeting creator and lead actor Aziz Ansari. Initially, her character was meant to be played by a straight white woman and be a potential love interest for Aziz. But after meeting her, it became clear that what the show needed was Lena, playing her authentic self. "All of us actors play heightened versions of ourselves. I don't know if we've seen a sly, harem-pants-wearing, cool-Topshop-sweatshirt-wearing, snapback-hat-rocking lesbian on TV," she said. "I know how many women I see out in the world who are very much like myself."

"We exist. To me, the visibility of it was what was going to be so important and so exciting."

Sharing Her Truth

She didn't dream of being an actor. From an early age, Lena committed to the idea of being a television writer. But when she got to Hollywood, it became clear that she was never meant to play one role; she was meant to call the shots. When accepting her Emmy, Lena talked about the importance of diversity in our entertainment and culture at large. "The things that make us different—those are our superpowers," she said. She urged viewers who feel outside of the mainstream to don a superhero cape every day "and go out there and conquer the world. It would not be as beautiful as it is if we weren't in it." Make no mistake, it's not just about representation; it's about implementing long-lasting change both on screen and off screen, in Hollywood and everyday life.

> "Go out there and conquer the world.
> It would not be as beautiful as it is
> if we weren't in it."

"I have a ton of mentees," she stated, in an interview with *Vanity Fair*. "They're all people of color. Some of them are poor. And I'm just trying to help them learn how to be great writers; and for those that have become really good writers, I help them get representation; and those that have representation, I want to help get them jobs. That to me is a form of activism. I was doing this before Time's Up was created. I am doing it now. Activism is me paying for a writer to go to a television-writing class."

She has no use for gatekeepers, and has used the weight behind her name to bring people into the industry and support their growth. Now, she's pitching mandates to address the systemic racism in entertainment. "It should feel taboo to be on a set that is not inclusive. If you are at a board meeting at a major network or a studio, and it's not inclusive, you should feel uncomfortable," she said in an interview with *Hollywood Reporter*. "Until that is the feeling, we won't make change. The reason I'm pitching mandates, hitting people in their pockets, is because I know that's what matters. Money is power."

Gina Yashere

A vibrant engineer and comedian

As a little girl growing up in east London, Gina Yashere was known for speaking her mind. She was born in Nigeria, and as a child emigrated to the UK with her family. Like many immigrants, her parents left everything behind, including their careers; in Nigeria, her mother was a school principal, and her father an academic. However, in England, their experience and intellect counted for little. Rather than accept a future of working menial jobs, her mother decided to change course and enter the world of entrepreneurship, whereas her father left the family and moved back to Nigeria when Gina was three.

Racism saturated her childhood. While in elementary school, a white man saw her leaning up against his parked vehicle and started screaming racial profanities. Instead of shrinking away in fear, she shouted right back. But he wasn't done. He physically assaulted Gina, repeatedly punching and kicking her in front of a teacher. He was caught, but justice was not served; the police let him off with a warning. Unsatisfied with the decision, Gina's mother decided to pursue a private prosecution. During the trial, it came out that the assailant was a firefighter, and the judge gave him an absolute discharge. The verdict painted a picture that Gina would never forget; justice was racialized.

Coping Through Humor

In high school, Gina began using her first name, Regina, and using humor to deal with racism rather than fighting. But it amplified the bullying and ridicule she was experiencing from those around her. When she was walking home from school one day, another student leaned out of the classroom window and yelled "Regina Vagina." Overwhelmed with rage, Gina ran up to the classroom and fought the girl. That day changed the course of her life. She was expelled. After a year of studying at home, she was invited back to school but Gina said "no, thanks." That year away had given her the space to grow into her personality. Equipped with a new wardrobe, regained confidence, and uncanny humor, she chose to attend a different school and reinvent herself. It worked; according to Gina, she's been cool ever since.

"Whenever I do interviews, they always go 'Is it difficult being a female comedian in a male environment?'"

After completing her A-levels exams, Gina became the only female engineer in her department. It's a period of her life that prepared her for her experience in comedy. "Whenever I do interviews, they always go 'Is it difficult being a female comedian in a male environment?' and I go: 'I worked on building sites with guys who used to hang pictures of monkeys above my overalls and stick bananas in my pockets, so no, compared to that, this is a walk in the park.' It built up my layers of resilience going through all those things," she said. When she started fantasizing about pushing her abuser down an elevator shaft, she decided it was time to quit. She chose to pursue comedy.

She had no experience, and truthfully didn't even care for the genre. However, in a few short months, she was runner-up in the 1996 Hackney Empire New Act of the Year competition and was featured on television. The audience loved her sets. Her secret? Drawing from her own experiences in everyday life. Gina was a hit. Her routines explored the cultural difference among African and Afro-Caribbean communities. Then came the racism. White comedians were being given primetime slots over Gina, even though their shows sold significantly fewer tickets. When she performed on *Mock The Week*, a producer asked her to slip into her Nigerian accent more during her shows, because the audience loved it. So, she did it to please them. "Then I got lambasted. People said: 'All she talks about is being African and black.'"

> *"I thought this is not how I should be feeling; I should not be coveting another black comic's success."*

The final straw came when another comedian was given their own show, an opportunity Gina had been vying for. She wanted to be happy for her, but because minority comedians were fighting for crumbs, it was difficult to feel anything other than jealousy. "I thought this is not how I should be feeling; I should not be coveting another black comic's success. We should all be able to be successful together, just like white comics were allowed to be. Then the BBC had the gall to come and ask me to help write on her show," she said in an interview with *The Guardian*. "I was like: OK, these guys are taking me for a fool, I'm out of here. I've got to get out of this country before I end up killing myself; by eating myself from the inside out and dying of a stroke or heart attack through bitterness and anger."

In Due Time

Gina would have her moment. Shortly after this experience, she decided that was enough—she didn't want to be anyone's token anymore and recommitted to doing the work that mattered to her. When she was first approached by *Bob Hearts Abishola*, she assumed she would be exploited again, and even asked her agent to turn down the offer. Her loved ones convinced her otherwise. "My younger brother, Edwin, and best friend, Lila, called me up and screamed at me for two hours, going: 'Do you not realize this is the opportunity you've been waiting for? Get a life, Gina. You've been moaning about lack of opportunities and here's one in your lap.' And I was like: 'You're right, I'll give it a go.'" It was one of the best decisions she's ever made. Originally, she was brought in as a consultant on all things African, which sounded weird to her. Then she met with the team and decided otherwise. "Once I got in the room with the guys, I began to really like them. I could see that they were trying to make a really good show, and it wasn't really an exploitative thing," she said in an interview with Insider.

> *"You'd watch movies with African characters, and the actors were completely wrong."*

After consulting for a couple of days, she was promoted to cocreator. She eventually went on to become an executive producer, writer, and actress on the show. It was possibly one of the best decisions the show made. During its first season, *Bob Hearts Abishola*, was CBS's highest-rated new sitcom with over five million viewers consistently every week, though reviews have been mixed. Her decisions not only improved the quality of the show, but also opened the gate for more minority talent. "You'd watch movies with African characters, and the actors were completely wrong," she said. "Their style of dress was completely wrong, or you have an entire family and every one of them has got a different accent from a different country within Africa." In *Bob Hearts Abishola* she insisted that they cast a dark-complexioned, Nigerian actress to play Abishola because even when it came to African roles, she noticed that whiteness continued to be the standard.

Gina's career is a tribute to her relentless efforts and her refusal to accept the boxes society forces her into.

More than that, though, her legacy is a testament to what can happen when we hold the door open for those after us.

Sports

Simone Biles

Black gymnast magic

Every competition and practice, Simone Biles has one goal: to top her personal best. "I'm trying to be better than I was at the last meet, so I'm trying to beat myself," Biles told NBC television. "I'm doing things that were unimaginable to the sport, and even for myself ... I'm really excited because I feel like I've pushed my limits."

To date, those unimaginable elements that Simone has perfected are infamous, she has sprinkled Black Girl Magic across the world of gymnastics and continues to leave an indisputable legacy laced with her infectious energy and welcoming spirit.

After dominating at the junior elite level, Simone won her first U.S. and World titles in 2013. By 2015, she became the first woman to win three consecutive all-around titles, with a record setting 10 gold medals at the international competition. It's hard to believe that the illustrious athlete stumbled into her purpose by chance, but that's exactly how her story started. Or maybe, it was always fate.

Every Experience Holds the Key

Born in Columbus, Ohio, Simone Biles began her life determined to beat the odds stacked against her. "My biological mom was suffering from drug and alcohol abuse, and she was in and out of jail," she recalled in an interview with Katie Couric. "I do remember always being hungry and afraid." When she was three years old, she and her siblings were removed from their home and placed in foster care. Three years later, she was adopted by her grandparents and Simone was given a second chance at life. "Being separated from my biological mom and being placed in foster care before I officially got adopted by my grandparents, it just set me up for a better route in life," she said. "I feel like I wouldn't be where I am unless that turning point happened. I would still be Simone Biles, just not the Simone Biles the world knows. I believe everything happens for a reason." A few months later, Simone discovered the sport that would shape her life.

> *"I feel like I wouldn't be where I am unless that turning point happened. I would still be Simone Biles, just not the Simone Biles the world knows."*

She was six years old, and only a few months into living with her new adopted parents. Weather conditions forced her daycare to change the destination of their field trip. Instead of venturing to nearby marshlands, the children were taken to Bannon's Gymnastix. An energetic Simone took to tumbling and moving her body in ways that immediately captured the attention of long-time coach Aimee Boorman, who recalls marveling over her strength and natural flexibility. Even as a beginner, it was clear Simone was fearless and in her natural element. At six, she was already considered late to the sport. But fate is always right on time, so it all worked out. She quickly outgrew the beginner classes and, with unbelievable speed, she was ready to compete.

By middle school, Simone was training 20 hours a week. By the time she entered the 9th grade, she made one of the most critical decisions a young athlete could make—she bet on herself. For Simone, going all in meant trading in hallmark high school moments for longer hours at the gym. Suffice to say, the sacrifice more than paid off.

The young athlete began training upward of 35 hours a week. In a few short years, Biles solidified a sponsorship deal with Nike—an undeniable sign that the athlete had arrived.

Her Name Is Simone Biles, Address Her As Such

Simone wants you to know, she isn't the next Usain Bolt or Michael Phelps; she is the only Simone Biles. She's trained her way to the pinnacle of her sport with indescribable tenacity. However, like many Black women, her success has not been without criticism. The more records she broke, the louder the snarky remarks from her competitors grew. But with grace, grit, and an unwavering faith in her belonging, she stayed committed and unbothered.

In 2013, Biles made history as the first Black woman to win the all-around title at the World Gymnastic Championship. An Italian gymnast who placed 11th bitterly gave a video interview suggesting that Biles only won because of her skin color and not because she was the superior athlete.

In 2013, Biles made history as the first Black woman to win the all-around title at the World Gymnastic Championship.

During the interview, the Italian gymnast suggested that next time, she and her teammate would "paint" their skin Black so they could win, too. For Simone, this was a first. "I didn't really notice racism until 2013," Biles told *TODAY* cohost Hoda Kotb. "I was on a world scene, and what made the news was another gymnast saying that if we painted our skin Black maybe we would all win because I had beaten her out of the beam medal. And that was really the news, rather than me winning."

She's learned to use the criticism of those who cannot reach her heights as her fuel. Have you noticed the embellished goat on her leotard? There's a story behind that. After repeatedly defying the laws of physics with her intricate routines, breaking countless records, her position in the sport was clear: the greatest of all time (this is what GOAT stands for). But for certain athletes, Simone's success triggered insecurities rather than inspiring them to work harder. This is a phenomenon that's familiar to many Black women, and other women of color. Rather than dim her light, she embraced her wins, her power, and that Black Girl Magic. She decided to decorate her leotard to reflect her greatness. The hostile comments, passive aggressive anti-Blackness, and negative rhetoric from her competitors could never be enough to overpower her self-confidence or her ability to perform.

When the pandemic indefinitely postponed the Tokyo Olympic Games, many athletes fell into a state of shock, grief, and uncertainty, including Simone. A gymnast typically only takes a handful of days off in their career and, with gyms closed, Simone had nowhere to train. She had also announced that she would retire after the Tokyo Games, and now her plans were in limbo. In true Simone Biles fashion, the setbacks only propelled her into breakthroughs. During lockdown she spent her time perfecting yet another skill: the Yurchenko double pike vault. That's a roundoff onto a springboard, a backward dive onto the vaulting table, and two full backflips in the difficult pike position. This vault takes immense power and strength. According to sports commentators, she performed better than all of them. But then, right as the long awaited Tokyo Olympics games were set to begin, something changed; Simone had changed and it became apparent after the qualifiers. She fumbled her way through practices, and struggled to land on her feet. "I was not physically capable," she said in an interview with *The Cut*. Then she did the bravest thing she could—she chose herself.

Lifting As She Climbs

For Simone, stepping away from the Olympics sent a powerful message: Black women were choosing themselves. Although her decision to withdraw was supported by her coaches and her team, not everyone was as understanding. She was criticized for being selfish, for letting down the United States, and for disappointing her teammates. But even the criticism tells a story. Simone Biles is among the greatest athletes of all time. She's broken just about every world record in her sport, winning 25 world championship medals, 19 of them gold. She chose to withdraw from the games she spent years training for because she could not trust her body to land safely.

As an athlete, Simone has always represented more than just herself. In a sport that has historically lacked Black athletes and downplayed their success, she is redefining what it means to be a gymnast.

"Growing up, you don't see a lot of African American gymnasts." Biles recognized the successes and impact of Black gymnasts that paved the way for her, highlighting the influence of Gabby Douglas in her interview with Katie Couric. "I remember when Gabby Douglas won I was like, 'Oh my gosh, if she can do it, then I can do it.'" She's said that she hopes to do the same for other Black athletes. Her bold embrace of her own vulnerability has given those around her permission to do the same. That's what makes her truly remarkable. Her reign as the greatest gymnast of all time has changed the face of gymnastics around the globe, and the world has not seen the last of her magic just yet.

Naomi Osaka

Caught in the net

We connect to our power when we tell the truth, both to ourselves and those around us. In many ways, Black women have been denied this privilege. Caught in between the crushing weight of patriarchy and the debilitating effects of anti-Black racism, we are forced to bite our tongues and endure in more ways than one. The times, however, are changing.

The "strong Black woman" narrative is slowly, but surely, being retired and many of us are giving ourselves permission to be soft, vulnerable, and open. We are allowing ourselves to rest.

Naomi Osaka is one of the women leading this change. She is one of the best female tennis players of our time, and has made headlines for her tenacity both on and off the court.

During the 2021 French Open, Osaka posted a statement on Twitter indicating that she would not be doing any press conferences at the tournament. "I've often felt that people have no regard for athletes' mental health, and this rings very true whenever I see a press conference or partake in one," wrote Naomi.

She went on to say that athletes are forced to sit through intrusive press conferences that often question an athlete's abilities. Naomi wasn't refusing to do press conferences to be difficult; she was doing it to protect her well-being.

Black Mental Health Matters

Following her decision to withdraw from the French Open, citing concerns for her mental health. Naomi, a self-described introvert, opened up about her mental health struggles that began when she won the US Open in 2018. She scored the biggest win of her career, beating Serena Williams and becoming the first Japanese player to win a Grand Slam title.

However, rather than celebrate what should have been one of the most memorable moments of her young career, she was apologizing to the crowd. "I know that everyone was cheering for Serena, and I'm sorry it had to end like this," Osaka said during her on-court post match interview. "I just want to say thank you for watching the match."

Throughout the game, Naomi endured boos and jeers from the crowd of such intensity, that Serena ended up consoling the crying champion. Although the pair ended the match in a warm embrace, that game shaped Naomi's career in more ways than one.

She started to develop anxiety around press conferences and began wearing headphones in the hope of blocking out the negativity that she could hear from the crowd; but to no avail. In some ways, Naomi withdrawing from the French Open was her stepping into her power.

Naomi Osaka is the highest-paid female athlete in the world. Her reluctance to put her career above her mental well-being has empowered many around the world to open up and be vulnerable.

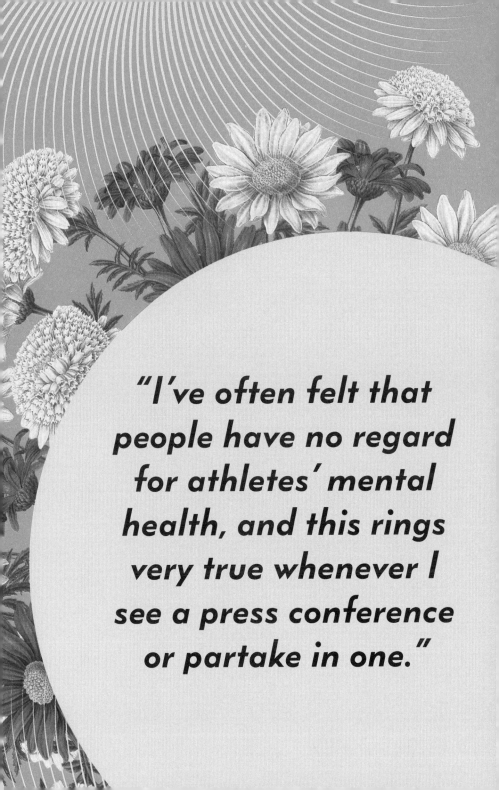

"I've often felt that people have no regard for athletes' mental health, and this rings very true whenever I see a press conference or partake in one."

And she's just getting started. Her decision to withdraw from the French Open made headlines, but it didn't deter her; she then subsequently withdrew from Berlin and Wimbledon. Then Netflix offered her a three-part series on her decision and the path to finding her voice.

During an early interview, Naomi told a reporter that she wanted "to be the very best, like no one ever was," then laughed and explained further, "I'm sorry; that's the Pokémon theme song. But, yeah, to be the very best, and go as far as I can go."

Redefining Success

In 1997, Naomi was born in Chūō-ku, Osaka, Japan, to a Haitian father and Japanese mother. When she was three, her family relocated to Long Island. Shortly after, her father enrolled Naomi and her sister in tennis lessons and nothing has ever been the same.

In 2019, she relinquished her US citizenship. Under Japanese law dual citizens are required to pick one citizenship by the time they turn 22 years old. For Naomi, the decision to give up her US citizenship was obvious. "I've been playing under the Japan flag since I was 14. It was never even a secret that I'm going to play for Japan for the Olympics," she said during an episode of her new self-titled docuseries on Netflix. "So I don't choose America and

"[I want] to be the very best, and go as far as I can go."

suddenly people are like, 'Your Black card is revoked.' And it's like, African American isn't the only Black, you know? I don't know, I feel like people really don't know the difference between nationality and race because there's a lot of Black people in Brazil, but they're Brazilian."

"I feel like people really don't know the difference between nationality and race."

Part of why Naomi chose to begin representing Japan and take on her mother's last name was to combat stereotypes of what it means to be Black and what it means to be Japanese. For Naomi, there's no choosing—she's both.

In all aspects of her career, Naomi has shown a continuous commitment to showing up on her own terms.

Caster Semenya

Up and running

Growing up, Caster Semenya played soccer every day after school and often in between classes. When she wasn't practicing her footwork, she was running long distances, sometimes even to neighboring villages. "I was always away from home, always in the bushes, and looking for adventures. So, my family always let me do what I like," she told the BBC in 2009. Her raw athleticism was apparent from an early age. Born in a remote South African village bordering Botswana, she did not have access to high-end training facilities, elite coaches, or proper running gear. But she had speed. In 2009, she won the African Junior Championships in the 800 and 1500 meter races with the times of 1:56.72 and 4:08.01, simultaneously breaking the 800 meter Senior and Junior South African records. Later that same year, Caster won gold in the 800 meter World Championships at just 18-years-old with a time of 1:55.45 in the final, setting the fastest time of the year. Then came the criticism.

Breaking the Mold

Prior to running in the World Championships in 2009, Caster's astounding speed prompted questions. She was simply too fast for some to comprehend. Rather than attribute her grace and athleticism to diligent training, critics took issue with her gender. To them, she was too masculine to compete in women's sports. "These kinds of people should not run with us," said Italian runner Elisa Cusma. "For me, she is not a woman. She is a man." But it wasn't just other competitors. *Time* magazine ran an article titled "Could This Woman's World Champ Be a Man?" The commentary was relentless, but it wasn't unfamiliar. There is a long history of Black women being vilified for their talents. As athletes, Black women are commonly masculinized, compared to animals, or robbed of their femininity in some capacity. Who could forget when Serena Williams was compared to a horse by the *LA Times*?

*"I was always away from home ...
and looking for adventures."*

In 2009, the International Association of Athletics Federation (IAAF) subjected Caster to a plethora of invasive body testing. Ignoring the fact that there was insufficient evidence to support the argument that higher testosterone levels would give Caster a competitive edge, she was prevented from competing throughout 2010. Although Caster was eventually cleared to compete in women's sports, the debacle cost her. Immediately following the IAAF's decision to test her hormone levels, her coach with Athletics South Africa (ASA), Wilfred Daniels, resigned, stating that he did not believe ASA advised Caster properly. He also apologized for being unable to protect her.

They Can't Stop Her

As much as the world tried to slow her down, Caster has simply refused to listen. She went on to win gold in the 800 meter in the 2012 and 2016 Olympics. Then the IAAF changed their rules; runners with testosterone above a certain level would have to take medication to lower it in order to compete against other women in the 400, 800, and 1500 meter events.

For Caster, this decision was unsurprising. "The IAAF has tried to slow me down for a decade, but this has actually made me stronger," she said in a statement to *The Washington Post*. "The decision of the CAS will not hold me back. I will once again rise above and continue to inspire young women and athletes in South Africa and around the world." By 2016, the IAAF suspended the policy on high natural levels of testosterone in women. That same year, Caster became the first person to win all three of the 400, 800, and 1500 meter titles at the South African National Championships. Not only did she walk away with three gold medals, she also set world leading times of 50.74 and 1:58.45 in the first two events, and a 4:10.93 in the 1500 meter, all within a nearly 4-hour span of each other.

When she was publicly questioned about her sex, her response was simply, "I am Mokgadi Caster Semenya. I am a woman and I am fast."

Growing up, she was nicknamed the Cobra because of her untouchable speed. But after years of enduring scrutiny laced with racism and sex-discrimination, Caster has shown that her talents go far beyond her abilities as an athlete.

Running has always symbolized freedom for Caster. When the world tried to take that from her, she simply refused.

.

Journalism

Koa Beck

A champion of women's equality

We've spent our lives surrounded by varying degrees of white feminism. It's in our literature, brand messaging, and between the covers of the magazines we grew up reading. It starts young, before we are even fully cognizant of our identity; Black girls are fed imagery that fuels the narrative that they are not the norm. How old were you the first time you realized that women who looked like you were erased by the suffragettes? Or that the 19th Amendment in the United States Constitution only gave white women the right to vote?

There are large swaths of history that are ignored in conversations and in our primary teachings not because they are contested factually but because they make some people uncomfortable. However, for others, these details are impossible to ignore.

Black Like Me

Koa Beck was born in Hawaii and raised in Los Angeles. She first became aware that she was racially ambiguous in the second grade. "My second-grade teacher had walked us through where to write our names in capital letters and what bubbles to fill in for our sex, our birth date, and ethnicity. But in the days before 'biracial' or 'multiracial' or 'choose two or more of the following,' I was confronted with rigid boxes of white or Black," she wrote in a personal essay for *Salon*.

Even at 8 years old, she knew that she was white passing. On the playground, the parents of her classmates often commented on her looks, describing her as striking and foreign. "Distant relatives on the white side of my family would remark that I could easily pass for Israeli, for Spanish, for Italian, and other nationalities that can be filed under pan-ethnic," she recalled. "But they always equated me with the culturally sanctioned 'chic' identities, like an exoticized princess you could encounter on a distant beach or in a novel."

As the years passed, Koa began to understand how her race and her sexuality dictated her experiences and ultimately limited the full expression of who she was. "I'm neither straight nor white, but I'm frequently mistaken for both—and it's taught me a lot about privilege," said Koa. "My privilege in passing reflects a racism and heterosexism that continues to flourish, despite romantic notions that racial mixing and gay marriage will create a utopian future free of prejudices. Police officers don't suspect me. Store owners like me. White strangers don't feel threatened by me. Racists get too comfortable with me. Homophobes unknowingly befriend me."

Rather than embrace the comfort and protection this afforded her, she used her experiences to address the shortcomings of white feminism. For Koa, one of the biggest disappointments with feminist theory was its Eurocentric approach to problem solving. "Feminism has been very good at indoctrinating women into white feminist principles, but also white feminist strategies," she said. "So, the idea that you just hurdle toward power, it doesn't matter in what capacity it will be used, it doesn't matter who you will have to exploit to get there—that ... in a systemic setting is progress, and is gender progress."

"Racism and heterosexism ... continues to flourish, despite romantic notions that racial mixing and gay marriage will create a utopian future free of prejudices."

Choosing Equality and Rejecting Privilege

Known for her sharp literary criticism, her work has appeared in *The Atlantic, Out, The Globe and Mail, TIME, The Guardian, Esquire, Vogue,* and *Marie Claire,* among others. Her short stories have been published in *Slice, Kalyani Magazine,* and *Apogee Journal.* She has been nominated for the Pushcart Prize and serves on the board of directors of *Nat.Brut,* an art and literary magazine, as well as on the advisory board of GALECA: The Society of LGBTQ Entertainment Critics.

"I'm neither straight nor white, but I'm frequently mistaken for both—and it's taught me a lot about privilege."

In 2019, Koa was awarded the Joan Shorenstein Fellowship at the Harvard Kennedy School, publishing an academic paper titled "Self-Optimization in the Face of Patriarchy: How Mainstream Women's Media Facilitates White Feminism." By 2021, she had released her long-awaited debut book, *White Feminism: From the Suffragettes to Influencers and Who They Leave Behind.*

"I tried to show in the book how feminism led by women of color and queer people does not have this end goal, and actually they are very suspicious of what we would think of as traditional power. It is in the foundational principle of their feminism to scrutinize that power and also to think about ways beyond it," said Koa.

In some ways, how she is perceived by others has become her reluctant alter ego. She has spent her entire adult life trying to break up with her white doppelganger, but it's proven to be unsuccessful.

148

Koa's living a life of "double consciousness," a term coined by eminent American sociologist W.E.B. Du Bois. "They look at me and always see their own," she wrote in an article for *Salon*. "Is it the presumed commonality that garnered me those interviews? Those smiles? Those callbacks? Those firm handshakes?"

These are the questions that Koa Beck has long sat with. While privilege was afforded to her from the earliest years of her life, she never embraced it. Did that matter? Was it enough that she asserted her Blackness and her queerness anytime she felt that they were questioned?

All of us are products of our circumstances. We do not choose the families we are born into, the communities we belong to, or the color of our skin. In many ways, we have no control over how society perceives us. But where we have control is in our choices and how we decide to use the advantages or disadvantages society prescribes to us at birth.

For Koa, rather than benefit from her proximity to whiteness, she chose to invest in the collective and challenge the impact white feminism has on women's liberation.

Nikole Hannah-Jones

The 1619 Project, and the truth that changed it all

In 2019, Nikole Hannah-Jones launched the 1619 Project, timed to coincide with the 400th anniversary of the beginning of American slavery. As part of this work, Nikole penned a deeply personal essay that argued that America was not a democracy until the civil rights struggle of Black Americans made it true. In 2020, she was awarded a Pulitzer Prize for commentary for her work on this project. Afterward she told *The New York Times'* staff it was "the most important work of my life."

It was a powerful, thought provoking, and highly researched piece that was well deserving of the applause. But it also pulled Nikole into a media frenzy. Critics of the piece were furious. The loudest critics were historians, who penned a letter to *The New York Times* criticizing the piece for "factual errors and the closed-door process behind it." Neither criticism had merit. She had been methodical in her research, and other historians had reported similar facts. Nikole was being criticized for the conclusions she reached, not for the quality or validity of her work. This was the silencing of a Black woman.

Writing Her Truth and Discovering Journalism

Nikole Hannah-Jones first discovered the power of her voice while she was a student at Waterloo West High. As an avid reader and news-enthusiast, she was regularly seen pouring through the pages of local newspapers and had a subscription to *The New York Times* long before her peers. One day, she was leafing through her high school paper and she noticed something missing. No one in those pages looked like her ...

She flipped through the entire paper and realized within those pages there were no Black students mentioned or photographed.

Shining Your Truth: Telling Stories That Matter

Confused and frustrated with the erasure, she complained to a trusted teacher. She felt unseen, and other Black students echoed the same sentiment. It was then that her teacher gave her advice that would become her north star. She was told there were options: she could continue to be consumed by the injustice, or she could change it by becoming a voice for truth.

It's safe to say Nikole picked the truth that day, and every day since. "I always understood that my charge as a Black journalist was to write about the Black experience, to report on my community and to report on the inequality that my community experiences," she said, in an interview with NPR. "That's why I became a journalist. I really wanted to excavate racial inequality." Keeping true to the promise she made to her high school teacher, she has long committed her career to bearing witness to stories that many have tried to ignore.

"That's why I became a journalist. I really wanted to excavate racial inequality."

In 2003, she began her career as an education reporter, focusing almost exclusively on segregation in America's public schools. "The thing about education being so important in the United States is that we were very early a country that decided that we believe in universal education. That if we were to be a great nation it couldn't just be the wealthy, it couldn't just be the powerful's children that would be able to get an education; that we had to be an educated society to be a democratic society," said Nikole, during a speech at the annual Power of Storytelling conference in Bucharest, Romania.

"We are one of the first nations that offered universal education to our children. And Horace Mann is considered the father of the American public school, and what he said is that education being on all of the devices of human origin is a great equalizer of the conditions of men. And in our country, we truly believe that. We believe that public education allows you—no matter where you come from, or who you are—to get going to the doors of the school and you will come out with the same education as someone who has much more money and much more power than you, and you can change a lot in life through education."

> *"It's hard to get people to care about poverty, because people feel like it won't change, that there's nothing you can do about it."*

Except she was seeing something very different. She saw an America with two philosophies on education: one for white students, and one for Black students. As she researched, she noticed a pattern—white students were being educated for democracy, and Black students were being educated for oppression. The color line she noticed as a child, while being bussed into her predominantly white school, still existed and it could be seen in resources, opportunities, and school conditions. But the problem was, no one really cared about education. At least not enough for her to spend the hours she needed to tell stories in ways that drove impact.

"It's hard to get people to care about poverty, because people feel like it won't change, that there's nothing you can do about it. That is just the way society is. And that is how school segregation was seen in the United States in 2013," said Nikole.

Finding Her Niche: Telling Stories With Impact

Committed to writing the stories that mattered, she set up a Google alert; she wanted to see every report and article that was being published on the state of public schools in America. Sometimes, several months would pass without a single article on the subject. Without a shadow of a doubt, she knew this was her beat. But she also knew that it would take a tremendous amount of work to convince her editors to allow her to spend months working on a project on school segregation, when it seemed like no one was interested. "What drives me is rage. Because I think what we're doing to children is wrong, and I'm not going to pretend to be objective about it. I think it's hypocritical and I think that it's wrong. I got into journalism because I feel like we have to do better and if we're not going to do better, I'm not going to let us sit comfortably and pretend that everything is OK."

When she tried to pitch an investigative piece on school segregation to *Atlantic* magazine, the editors rejected the pitch, telling her the story had already been told. So, she asked them to tell her the story and the room went quiet. "People think they know the story, but they actually don't. I think with a lot of the stories that we're trying to talk about—mass incarceration, poverty, war—we think we know the story," said Nikole. "Our job as storytellers—if we want to get people to care about things that seem to be fixed in our country—is we have to figure out a way to make them see the story in a different way and to help them understand that they actually don't know the story at all."

She developed a meticulous process for landing the stories she knew had to be told. By centering human voices, relying heavily on undeniable data, and trusting the fire in her belly, Nikole made a name for herself in a beat that has historically been overlooked.

"As storytellers ... we have to figure out a way to make [people] see the story in a different way and to help them understand that they actually don't know the story at all."

Go Where You Are Wanted, Stay Where You Are Valued

When Nikole was first accepted into the University of North Carolina at Chapel Hill's Master of Journalism program on a full-tuition scholarship, she could not believe her luck. She had been drawn to her alma mater since she was a little girl, and openly dreamed about one day walking the campus's illustrious halls.

"UNC ... provided the foundation for all that I would become. And through the years, Carolina has been so good to me; inviting me to give the journalism school's commencement address in 2017; honoring me with the Young Alumni Award that same year and he Distinguished Alumna Award in 2019; and last year, inducting me into the N.C. Media Hall of Fame," said Nikole.

Nearly two decades after graduating, she was offered a tenured teaching position at the school, as the Knight Chair in Race and Investigative Reporting. Few were surprised. Nikole was one of the most highly regarded and celebrated journalists in the country, and she was a constant presence at her alma mater. For her, joining the faculty of her beloved school was a powerful opportunity to help shape the next generation of journalists and formalize the mentorship she had long offered UNC students. Immediately, she said yes and began the months-long tenure process during which every aspect of her career was scrutinized. Unsurprisingly, the Pulitzer-winning journalist's candidacy was widely supported throughout the school. But she would never join the faculty at UNC.

Weeks shy from her first official lecture, Nikole was told that her application had been rejected by the Board of Trustees. Nine days later an article in the *N.C. Policy Watch* explained why. Her tenure wasn't denied because of her credentials, it was denied because of political influence.

The school was met with intense backlash, both on and off campus. Students expressed their pain and hurt, journalists from across the nation wrote letters supporting Nikole, and Black faculty members resigned in solidarity. Through all of this, Nikole watched the school she loved, the school she had given so much, refuse to acknowledge the truth.

"At some point when you have proven yourself and fought your way into institutions that were not built for you, when you've proven you can compete and excel at the highest level, you have to decide that you are done forcing yourself in," she wrote, in her statement announcing her decision to decline the tenure UNC eventually offered her.

"I fought this battle because I know that all across this country Black faculty, and faculty from other marginalized groups, are having their opportunities stifled, and that if political appointees could successfully stop my tenure, then they would only be emboldened to do it to others who do not have my platform. I had to stand up. And I won the battle for tenure."

"At some point ... when you've proven you can compete and excel at the highest level, you have to decide that you are done forcing yourself in."

Nearly a year after being offered a faculty position at UNC, Nikole accepted a position as the inaugural Knight Chair in Race and Reporting at Howard University.

As Nikole so eloquently said, "For too long, powerful people have expected the people they have mistreated and marginalized to sacrifice themselves to make things whole. The burden of working for racial justice is laid on the very people bearing the brunt of the injustice, and not the powerful people who maintain it. I say to you: I refuse."

Nikole is one of the most revered journalists of our time, and what's made her the force that she is, is her unwillingness to soften or bend the truth for anyone.

Abby Phillip

A compelling journalist

If you've ever watched Abby Phillip on television, one of the first things you'll notice is her presence. She was born to be on television, but it turns out it was never really part of her vision.

"I'm a print reporter at heart—I like doing the work. I like interviews. I like reporting. Earlier in my career, I had worked at a TV company and saw all of these big personalities, whether it was Diane Sawyer or George Stephanopoulos, or David Muir," she said in an interview with Gayle King for *The Cut*. "And I'm thinking to myself, I don't feel quite like that. I don't think I have a big personality."

She comes across as shy and quiet the first time you meet her, but she certainty isn't—she just keeps to herself. "And I'm not very attention-seeking; in fact, I am attention-averse in some ways," she said.

In the early days of her career, she pretended people weren't actually watching her. But the truth is, it was impossible not to. Her storytelling was just that compelling.

Finding Your Footing

When we enter a new chapter of our lives, often the adjustment period eats away at our confidence and fills us with doubt. Did we make the right decision? Do we belong? Little by little as you begin to make space for yourself, that feeling dissolves into belonging. For Abby, it was no different.

It took seven months of her working on air to truly begin to feel comfortable in front of a camera. "We have people who coach us on television performance, but I struggled with how you're supposed to talk in the news," she said. "It just wasn't comfortable for me. I don't have a TV background, I never did local news, I don't have a TV voice. It was not working for me to try to sound like other people."

So, she started speaking to her audience the way she would a friend, or a friendly neighbor. "I think people do want their news from authoritative sources, but they also want to understand you," she recounted. "They want you to speak in a way that feels familiar to them."

Abby quickly realized that as a Black journalist covering politics, she did not have the same access as her white counterparts.

On Being a Black Journalist

Abby began covering the Trump administration in 2017. Initially, she was concerned that she did not have enough background knowledge, or the right sources to cover the president adequately. But she was wrong. When it came to reporting on Trump, many reporters were chasing the stories that focused on his personal life, but Abby quickly

"The story is not just the gossip. The story is also about the bigger picture, about whether this administration is actually prepared to govern," she said.

realized that as a Black journalist covering politics, she did not have the same access as her white counterparts. However, what she lacked in political sources, she made up for in her insight and storytelling. "The story is not just the gossip. The story is also about the bigger picture, about whether this administration is actually prepared to govern," she said. "Because from the start, all the warning signs were there—the inability to tell the truth, the chaos of the administration, the lack of attention to policy-making, everything we saw develop over the next four years."

When the travel ban was put into place, it became clear that this was an administration that did not understand how to govern the nation. For Abby, that was the real story behind the headlines and the focal point she chose to lead with.

Instead of concentrating on the adversity she faced, how her race often prevented her from being in the right room at the right time and walking away with the "scoop" all journalists dream of: she chose to pivot and focus on the story others were missing.

*"Because they come to me last,
I can't say the obvious thing, because
that's already been said by three
other people."*

Twice as Hard, Twice as Good

Abby's gusto, instincts, and clarity make her a phenomenal journalist. As a Black woman, it also painted a target on her back. In 2018, she was in a scrum with several journalists when she asked then-President Donald Trump a very direct question. He paused, tilted his head, and said "What a stupid question that is." Of course, the question was anything but; it came shortly after Trump fired Jeff Sessions, the attorney general, and replaced him with Matt Whitaker. She asked if he wanted Whitaker to rein in the Mueller investigation, a question that undoubtedly made Trump uncomfortable.

"I remember being surprised, because he had not reacted to me like that before. But after that aired, I got calls and texts from girlfriends and colleagues, especially my Black female friends," she said. "They were furious about it because of the implication of him telling a Black woman that she's stupid. I know that what he said is not true, and I don't take things like that personally, particularly from this president who has such a long history of insulting people. I don't get my self-esteem from Donald Trump or any other politician, frankly."

Like most women of color, Abby has learned to use the experiences meant to demoralize her to her advantage. During panels, and news scrums, politicians often answer her question last, if at all. "And because they come to me last, I can't say the obvious thing, because that's already been said by three other people," she said.

Abby had two options: become a wallflower and remain silent or ask tougher, more nuanced questions. She chose the latter, and it helped make her a rising star at CNN and in the world of journalism. Early in 2021, the network announced that Abby would be the new host for *Insider Politics*, replacing veteran journalist John King.

> *By not allowing others to place limits on her, Abby has paved her own way and is leaving her mark in the world, one story at a time.*

Elaine Welteroth

Defining her own success

When Elaine Welteroth first started her career, she would slick her hair back into tight low buns before interviews. Like many young Black professionals, she was concerned her hair would be a distraction or deemed unprofessional and messy. Growing up in a mixed-race family, she had always felt a little bit uncomfortable; like she didn't fit into this world.

"My very first memory in life is being in preschool, surrounded by a sea of white kids and being assigned a family collage project. The teachers gave us magazines, and everyone started flipping through those pages and started working on their collage. I'm still flipping and I'm realizing that no one looks like me, or my mom, or my brother," she recounted during a segment of *The Talk*.

"There were plenty of white dad options, but in that moment it made me realize for the first time that I was different and I immediately felt ashamed. I felt embarrassed for being different and I felt like being different made me less than. I just remember looking around and thinking that maybe if I started doing what everyone else was, they wouldn't notice I was different."

She started cutting out white faces from the magazines and made a collage of a white family instead of one that represented her own. "It was so awkward for everyone. The teachers tried to jump in with their magazines but there was no representation at the time," she said. "When I came home, my mother took one look at that white paper family and she made us sit down at the table as a family and redo the assignment together with *Ebony* and *Essence* magazines."

Her mother took that family collage and hung it in Welteroth's room. For years, it was the first thing she saw every morning and it helped reshape how she understood her place in this world.

As she advanced through her career, her relationship with her hair began to change. Whereas initially, she was hesitant to wear her natural curls, she began to understand the importance of owning her Blackness.

This was a drastic change, both internally and externally. "It represented a point of difference. And if I was bold enough to walk into an interview with my hair as it is naturally, I think it says something about my confidence, and my ability to think outside the box, and to be who I am no matter what," she said in an interview with Forbes.

"And in the right corporate culture, in the right environment, that's an asset. And that's the kind of environment I want to be in."

Breaking the Mold and Leaving Her Mark

In 2017, she made Condé Nast history and became the youngest editor-in-chief in the company's 108-year history, at 29 years old. It was a remarkable rise in a remarkable career; in under a decade, Welteroth rose from intern to editor-in-chief. Championed by fashion industry favorites, she was more than deserving of the promotion. In a single year, she helped grow *Teen Vogue*'s website traffic from 2.7 million to 9.2 million unique visitors a year, with print subscriptions reportedly up 535% in a year. She had earned this, but others thought otherwise.

> *"There were plenty of white dad options, but in that moment it made me realize for the first time that I was different."*

"I worked hard to get a dream job, then found out in the headlines that in fact I had become a Black woman making history," she said in an interview with *The Guardian*. "Because the headlines just made it seem like I was a sort of token Black hire, which feeds into this magical negro complex, right? All you need is one token black person and then they can transform the whole thing. And I don't want to be a part of selling lies about success."

The fact that anyone could see a *New York Times* bestselling author and award-winning journalist as anything other than deserving is a difficult concept to digest. But it's also one she's learned to expect.

"I think anyone who's accomplished any amount of success, especially a woman, especially a woman of color, if they tell you they do not struggle with self-doubt on any level on any day, they're lying to you. It's just par for the course," she said to Forbes.

"And I think no matter what level of success you achieve, you will still feel that. I think it's important to normalize those feelings and to not stay stuck in them, because tomorrow's a new day."

Welteroth has learned that success isn't dependent on what people say, but on liberation and living a life feeling free to own all of who you are.

"I hope that young women feel like they can do freakin' anything. Because they can. No matter where they came from, no matter what their life looks like today, they get to decide where they want to be, and they get to redefine that along the way. There is no singular definition of success."

> *"I worked hard to get a dream job, then found out in the headlines that in fact I had become a Black woman making history."*

But regardless of how you define success, Elaine Welteroth fits the criteria. At *Teen Vogue*, her time as editor-in-chief fundamentally reshaped the magazine by focusing on issues affecting teens and prioritizing political and social change over trends.

After the 2016 election, the magazine published the video "These Nine Young People Have Some Words for Donald Trump." From migrant issues and racial justice, to international affairs and the power of social media, Welteroth fundamentally reshaped the magazine by creating spaces for social issues that largely went ignored before her time as editor-in-chief.

Go Where You're Called and Honor Your Rhythm

After transforming the culture and influence of *Teen Vogue*, Welteroth resigned from the magazine and from Condé Nast.

Many were surprised; even Welteroth questioned whether she had made the right decision. But she has not looked back once.

"People get stuck when they feel fear because they think maybe it's a sign that they're not ready. But I think that anything that you do that's worth doing will elicit fear. It's part of the process, and I think you just have to make friends with fear—that's advice that Ava Duvernay gave me—when she swooped in and mentored me during that actual career transition, and she's right," she said in an interview with *Elle Magazine*.

"You gotta make friends with fear and learn how to dance with fear, and without fail, what I've learned and what I've seen, is that your most transformative work will happen on the other side of fear. But you gotta make the jump."

Since leaving *Teen Vogue,* Welteroth moved from New York to California and has made the transition into television as a judge on *Project Runway,* and a cohost for *The Talk*.

She's also published her memoir, *More Than Enough: Claiming Space for Who You Are (No Matter What They Say)*.

What makes Welteroth's career so remarkable is her ability to utilize every experience, both personal and professional, as well as each critic and mentor as a stepping stone for bigger and bolder dreams.

"When the world tells you to shrink ... expand."

Food and Drink

Dominique Crenn

The culinary entrepreneur

Dominique Crenn was 21 years old when she decided to be a chef. She had traveled extensively through Europe in the years before and learned about the endless styles of cooking, especially with the limitless possibilities with ingredients from each culture. She was in love, and like any great love story, Dominique's passion would require sacrifice. Her dream of becoming a chef in France was almost impossible; most if not all kitchens were run by men, and they were certainly not interested in a woman taking up their space. Rather than melt into the background and bid farewell to the dream, she decided to seek greener pastures. She packed up all her belongings and walked away from the life that she knew, choosing to resettle in California.

Coming Alive: On Chasing Her Dreams

The moment she arrived in San Francisco, she was home. Slowly, and then all at once her dreams began to fall into place. Dominique began her formal training as a chef and built an impressive résumé over the next nine years, bringing her unique cooking style to some of the city's most lauded restaurants. Her first two years on the city's culinary scene were spent under the mentorship of San Francisco luminaries Jeremiah Tower and Mark Franz. She then brought her talents to the highly acclaimed restaurants Campton Place, 2223 Market, and the Park Hyatt Grill. She was subsequently hired as executive chef of the Yoyo Bistro at the Miyako Hotel where she obtained an impressive three-star review in the annual *Access San Francisco* book during her one-year stint at the restaurant. For nearly a decade, she absorbed everything the city had to offer. After a period of time, she chose to discover the tastes of Indonesia and eventually make history.

In 1997, Dominique became the first-ever female executive chef in Indonesia, heading the kitchen at the InterContinental Hotel in Jakarta. It was at this kitchen that she won her first Michelin star. With a new palette, refined skills, and leadership experience, she returned to California and spent the next eight years as the executive chef of Manhattan Country Club in Manhattan Beach.

Today, she is the co-owner and chef of the three-Michelin-starred restaurant Atelier Crenn in San Francisco, where artistry is at the forefront, cuisine is a craft, and the community is an inspiration. Dominique is the first female chef in the US to receive three Michelin Stars.

> *"Although food is universal, people are discriminated against not only for the color of the skin, but also for the way they cook."*

Discrimination In the Restaurant Industry

In 2011, Dominique decided she wanted to open a restaurant that was founded on community and a sense of belonging. From the moment she stepped foot in San Francisco, she knew the city was different. It was when she moved back to California that she opened Atelier

Crenn, with the commitment to make every guest and staff member feel like family. For Dominique, cooking has always been about freedom. However, she still struggled with external voices trying to define her. "When I was opening Atelier Crenn, I did this interview with a women's magazine," she said. "They wanted me to do a photo shoot and look like a housewife. I was really confused about it, so they did my hair and all that, and I was just so ashamed of the picture. It wasn't me. And I realized at that moment that they wanted to put me in a box. Although food is universal, people are discriminated against not only for the color of the skin, but also for the way they cook." For Dominique, as a queer biracial Black woman, this was a familiar experience. She had spent her entire life avoiding labels and looking for spaces where she could simply exist as herself.

*"I always believed that the way
the world needs to evolve is
with diversity."*

"I always believed that the way the world needs to evolve is with diversity. Different voices bring amazing ideas. Let's not be silent and complicit anymore."

Nadiya Hussain

A legend in the baking

Nadiya Hussain watched the first four seasons of *The Great British Baking Show* (*The Great British Bake Off*) with her husband, and after the first few episodes they were hooked. Each viewing followed a similar pattern: "I would sit quietly and observe techniques and get familiar with alien baking terms. He would sit through each episode and shout at the box 'Nadiya you can do that!' And I would ignore him," she recalled.

Then one day toward the end of season four, he gave her something that would change her life. It was an application to *The Great British Bake Off* Season 6 in the UK. But she refused to apply. "I gave him one look and said 'no way.' For over 20 years I suffered with panic disorder and he was the one who saw the worst of it," she said.

"He was the one who propped me up every time I willed myself to fail. 'I think you should do this,' he said. 'Your wings were clipped somewhere along the way but I think it's time for you to fly.' So I entered Bake Off because he was right. I had lost myself in the madness that is life. I was everything—a daughter, a sister, a wife, a mother—but I still was nowhere near finding me."

Bullying and Mental Health

Growing up was not easy for Nadiya; the daughter of Bangladeshi immigrants, life was a constant struggle of trying to find her footing in a world that didn't seem to want her. At school, she was bullied for her complexion and her religion. "They would wait in corners and pull chunks of my hair out, until I was bleeding," she recalled. During her last year of elementary school, she recalls a number of classmates flushing her head in the toilet. "I still have the memory of the water going up my nose and thinking, 'If they don't pull me up now, I am going to drown,'" she said. "They eventually stopped and I had my first ever panic attack."

"They would wait in corners and pull chunks of my hair out, until I was bleeding."

By ten years old she was certain she wanted to die. She remembers hearing about suicide on TV and thinking, "What? I can buy this ticket and I can just go and I'd never get bullied again? I didn't know what death was. All I knew was that it meant not living the life I had now—and I didn't like my life," she wrote in her autobiography *Finding My Voice.* "I was excited that I was going to do this. I was not going to get bullied tomorrow."

The plan was set. She came home from school one day with the intention of overdosing on pills, but her plan was interrupted. After swallowing the first tablet, she realized she needed more water and walked out into her living room to find her family surrounding her mother. There was news—her mother was having another child. Nadiya was going to be a big sister again. She decided to go through with her plan after the baby was born. "I had to meet this new baby who was either my brother or sister," she wrote. However, after meeting her baby brother she said that she fell so in love with him that she chose to live. "I can't go anywhere," she thought, "I have to stay for him. He will need me. So I stayed. The epitome of a new life in more ways than one." That meant facing her bullies.

Getting Help

Like many people who grew up with mental health issues, Nadiya didn't know there was a word for how overwhelmed she felt. She also didn't know that she could ask for help. At 14 she was diagnosed with anxiety and panic disorder. She began cognitive behavioral therapy for treatment but was unable to continue for financial reasons.

"Growing up I had a brother and sister who were really poorly, literally on death's door. It felt daft for me to go to my parents and say, 'I'm feeling a bit panicked.' 'What about?' 'Don't know,'" she said. "Saying it out loud as a child is scary, but saying I felt unstable out loud as an adult with children was really scary. The fear of losing your children stops you from saying anything. It's a never-ending battle." Then, at 26, she decided that things weren't okay and that she needed help."

"I went to the doctor and within 10 minutes he'd given me pills. I took them and I felt nothing. Numb. When the kids did a nice painting at nursery, I felt nothing," she said. "When they fell over, nothing. I thought, 'This can't be good.' I came off the medication even though the doctor said I shouldn't and that's when I discovered walking."

> *"I'm my own worst enemy, but I'm my own treatment, too."*

She started walking up to 4 miles (7 km) every day, so that she could feel good in her body and in her mind. "I've spent my whole life not trusting myself. But when you give yourself the right tools you realize you're the only person you can trust to look after yourself," she said. "I'm my own worst enemy, but I'm my own treatment, too."

Staying Resilient

When Nadiya won *The Great British Baking Show* (*The Great British Bake Off*), a nation was moved to tears. As she was being crowned she vowed, "I'm never going to put boundaries on myself ever again. I'm never going to say I can't do it." It was more than just a show for Nadiya, it was an opportunity to rediscover the little girl she never got to be. She's used her platform to speak up on the issues that she felt forced to stay quiet about in the past. "I now work in an industry that's very ... Caucasian, male, and there I am—a five foot one Muslim brown girl, and it's not my world," said Nadiya in an interview with the *Radio Times* magazine. "We have to question why there aren't more people of color working in television, publishing, and the hospitality industry."

"I'm never going to put boundaries on myself ever again. I'm never going to say I can't do it."

Nadiya is no stranger to experiencing racism. After winning *The Great British Baking Show* (*The Great British Bake Off*), Nadiya says she's experienced more racism in the last five years than ever before. "I haven't always thought there's space for me. But I tell myself and my kids, 'Keep your elbows out.' My grandad started it when he moved to the UK from Bangladesh and was beaten by racists. If he'd given up and gone back home, we wouldn't be here today. This is why I say it's more than just about baking for me, it's about finding a place for me in this industry."

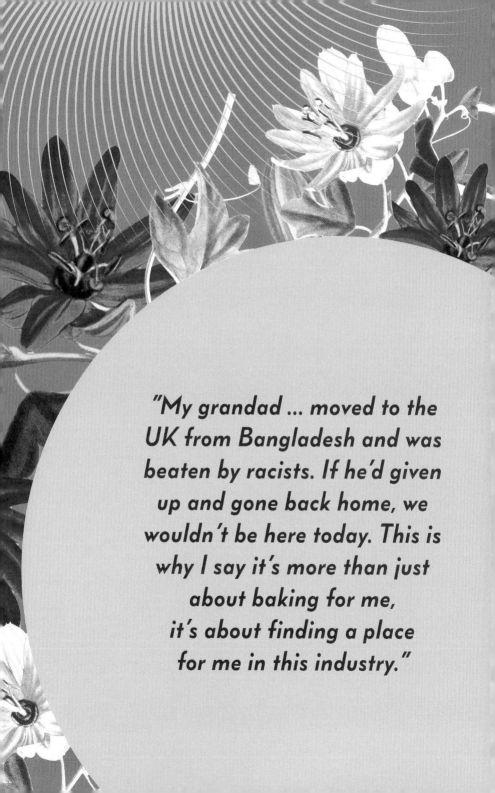

"My grandad ... moved to the UK from Bangladesh and was beaten by racists. If he'd given up and gone back home, we wouldn't be here today. This is why I say it's more than just about baking for me, it's about finding a place for me in this industry."

Index

Sources and Credits

General: www.abcnews.go.com; www.americanbazaaronline.com; www.bbc.com; www.biography.com; www.bloomberg.com; www.britannica.com; www.buzzfeednews.com; www.cbsnews.com; www.cnn.com; www.eastbaytimes.com; www.forbes.com; www.foxnews.com; www.thegazette.co.uk; www.goodreads.com; www.theguardian.com; www.hollywoodreporter.com; www.huffpost.com; www.latimes.com; www.nbcsports.com; www.nytimes.com; www.oprahdaily.com; www.politico.com; www.reuters.com; www.salon.com; www.telegraph.co.uk; www.thetimes.co.uk; www.universalsports.com; www.usatoday.com; www.vanityfair.com; www.vogue.com; www.washingtonpost.com; www.youtube.com;

Abby Phillips www.thecrimson.com; www.thecut.com; www.foxnews.com; www.publishersweekly.com; www.washingtonian.com;
Dr. Alaa Murabit www.alaamurabit.com; www.earthbeat.sk.ca; www.unwomen.org; www.womendeliver.org;
Amanda Gorman www.bostonglobe.com; www.glamour.com; www.independent.co.uk; www.newsweek.com; www.poetryfoundation.org; www.tatler.com;
Angelica Ross www.brainyquote.com; www.cassiuslife.com; www.crowdmgmt.com; www.pinknews.co.uk; www.self.com; www.tvovermind.com;
Arundhati Bhattacharya www.financialexpress.com; www.firstpost.com; www.moneycontrol.com; www.telegraphindia.com; www.timesofindia.indiatimes.com;
Ava DuVernay www.avaduvernay.com; www.billboard.com; www.thecut.com; www.essence.com; www.filmmakermagazine.com; www.insider.com; www.interviewmagazine.com; www.latinpost.com; www.metacritic.com; www.rogerebert.com; www.vulture.com;
Caster Semenya www.thehindu.com; www.sahistory.org.za; www.worldathletics.org;

Darnella Frazier www.dailydot.com; www.newyorker.com; www.pulitzer.org; www.seattletimes.com; www.usatoday.com;
Dominique Crenn www.culinaryepicenter.com; www.longreads.com; www.vegnews.com; www.theworlds50best.com;
Dolores Huerta www.doloreshuerta.org; www.npr.org;
Elaine Welteroth www.elainewelteroth.com;
Gabby Riviera www.avclub.com; www.gabbyrivera.com; www.hnmagazine.com; www.themarysue.com; www.psychologytoday.com; www.questia.com; www.remezcla.com; www.vulture.com; www.womenwriteaboutcomics.com;
Gina Yashere www.businessinsider.com; www.ginayashere.com; www.hometownlife.com; www.montrealmirror.com;
Issa Rae www.glamour.com; www.imdb.com; www.pagesix.com; www.sheleadsafrica.org; www.time.com;
Kamala Harris www.montrealgazette.com; www.sfgate.com; www.whitehouse.gov;
Kehlani www.billboard.com; www.bustle.com; www.elle.com; www.thefader.com; www.kehlani.com; www.latina.com; www.rollingstone.com; www.vulture.com; www.wmagazine.com;
Dr. Kizzmekia Corbett www.blackhealthmatters.com; www.healthtalk.unchealthcare.org; www.nationalgeographic.com; www.newsoforange.com;
Koa Beck www.koabeck.com; www.lithub.com;
Lena Waithe www.chicagomag.com; www.chicagotribune.com; www.emmys.com; www.fastcompany.com; www.womenandhollywood.com;

Mae Jemison www.rediff.com; secondwavemedia.com; www.womenshistory.org;

Malala Yousafzai www.malala.org; www.nobelprize.org;

Michaela Coel www.bafta.org; www.bfi.org.uk; www.interviewmagazine.com;

Michelle Obama *Becoming* (autobiography); www.essence.com; www.history.com; obamawhitehouse.archives.gov;

Nadiya Hussain www.belfasttelegraph.co.uk; www.bbcgoodfood.com; www.comedy.co.uk; www.goodhousekeeping.co.uk; www.heraldscotland.com; www.irishnews.com; www.metro.co.uk; www.nadiyahussain.com; www.oxfordtimes.co.uk; www.radiotimes.com; www.yorkshirepost.co.uk; www.yourhomemagazine.co.uk;

Naomi Osaka www.businesstraveller.com; www.cincinnati.com; www.japantimes.co.jp; www.straitstimes.com; theconversation.com; www.tennis.com; www.tennisviewmag.com; www.wtatennis.com;

Nikole Hannah-Jones www.nikolehannahjones.com;

Dr. Sima Samar www.gg.ca; www.msmagazine.com; www.rightlivelihood.org; www.un.org;

Simone Biles www.facebook.com (Versus Series - What Can't I Do?); www.insider.com; www.people.com; www.popsugar.co.uk; www.teenvogue.com; www.today.com;

Sônia Guajajara globalshakers.com; www.huckmag.com; www.nobordersnews.org; www.survivalinternational.org;

Stacey Abrams www.blog.ted.com; www.fortune.com; www.glamour.com; www.staceyabrams.com;

The publisher would like to thank the following for their kind permission to reproduce their photographs:
(Key: a-above; b-below/bottom; c-center; f-far; l-left; r-right; t-top)

Alamy Stock Photo: dani codina 90, CTK 138, Julian Guadalupe 144, Dinendra Haria 96, Juergen Hasenkopf 132, Image Press Agency 102, Newscom 12, 126, Sipa US 16, 164, UPI 108; Getty Images: Emily Assiran 28, Robyn Beck / AFP 158, Billboard Music Awards 2021 40, Chen Xiaomei / South China Morning Post 48, Aaron J. Thornton / Getty Images for ESSENCE 118, Rich Fury / Getty Images for dcp 114, Earl Gibson III 78, Ira L. Black / Corbis 70, Louise Kennerley / Fairfax Media 82, Jon Kopaloff / FilmMagic 62, Emma McIntyre 22, Stefano Montesi / Corbis 74, Tim Nwachukwu / The New York Times 52, Daniel Zuchnik / Getty Images for NYCWFF 172; Library of Congress, Washington, D.C.: Renee Bouchard 34; NASA: 58; Shutterstock.com: Roger Askew / The Oxford Union 86, Ken McKay / ITV 176, John Minchillo / AP 150; Marvin Joseph: Nicole Ellis illustrated by Natasha Cunningham 190, Khristina Godfrey 191

US Cover images: Front: Alamy Stock Photo: CTK cl, Dinendra Haria cr, Juergen Hasenkopf tr, Sipa US br, UPI tc; Getty Images: Tim Nwachukwu / The New York Times bl; Library of Congress, Washington, D.C.: Chuck Kennedy tl; NASA: bc; Back: Alamy Stock Photo: dani codina c, Newscom l; Getty Images: Stefano Montesi / Corbis r
UK Cover images: Front: Alamy Stock Photo: CTK cl, Dinendra Haria cr, Juergen Hasenkopf tr, Sipa US br, UPI tc; Getty Images: Tim Nwachukwu / The New York Times bl; Library of Congress, Washington, D.C.: Chuck Kennedy tl; NASA: bc; Back: Alamy Stock Photo: Newscom l; Getty Images: Stefano Montesi / Corbis r; Shutterstock.com: Ken McKay / ITV c

All other images © Dorling Kindersley

About the Author

Nicole Ellis is a journalist and a digital anchor for *PBS NewsHour*. Nicole previously worked at *The Washington Post*, covering social issues as well as hosting and directing original documentaries and breaking news videos for *The Post*'s website and social media channels, for which she received an Emmy nomination in 2017. Her documentary series, *Should I Freeze My Eggs?* won the 2019 Digiday Publishers Award. She also created and hosted the Webby Award–winning news literacy series *The New Normal*, the most viewed video series in the history of *The Washington Post*'s, *The Lily*. She is also the host of Critical Conversations on BookClub, an author-led book club platform. For more information on Nicole, please visit her website: www.nicoleellis.co.

About the Illustrator

Natasha Cunningham is a Graphic Designer and Visual Artist from Kingston, Jamaica. She's spent the last decade working in branding, advertising, and print design. Today, she creates portrait-focused digital collages for her ongoing series, "A Portrait Design A Day," which serves as an exploration of her love for digital collages and storytelling. Natasha has had the opportunity to work with Adobe, Netflix, and the *Oprah Magazine*, to name a few. For more information on Natasha, please visit her website: https://natashashaneek.com/

Senior Editor Elizabeth Cook
US Senior Editor Megan Douglass
Editor Beth Davies
Senior Designer Lauren Adams
Designer Lisa Sodeau
Production Editor Marc Staples
Production Controller Louise Daly
Acquisitions Editor Pete Jorgensen
Managing Art Editor Jo Connor
Publishing Director Mark Searle

DK would like to thank the author Nicole Ellis, the illustrator Natasha Cunningham,
Jo Walton for picture research, Sharan Dhaliwal for copy-editing,
and Vanessa Bird for index creation.

First published in Great Britain in 2022 by
Dorling Kindersley Limited
DK, One Embassy Gardens, 8 Viaduct Gardens,
London SW11 7BW

The authorised representative in the EEA is
Dorling Kindersley Verlag GmbH. Arnulfstr. 124,
80636 Munich, Germany

Page design copyright © 2022 Dorling Kindersley Limited
A Penguin Random House Company
10 9 8 7 6 5 4 3 2 1
002– 326327–September/2022

Text copyright © Nicole Ellis 2022

A CIP catalogue record for this book is available from the British Library.

ISBN: 978-0-2415-3173-0

Printed and bound in China

For the curious

www.dk.com

This book was made with
Forest Stewardship Council™
certified paper—one small
step in DK's commitment
to a sustainable future.